BRAVE CREATIVE HUMAN

EMBRACE ~~FAILURE~~, *← FAILURE*
REFRAME IMPOSTER SYNDROME,
AND BE UNAPOLOGETICALLY YOU

DIANA VARMA

Copyright © 2025 by Diana Varma

All rights reserved. No part of this publication may be reproduced, stored in a retrieval system, or transmitted in any form or by any means, electronic, mechanical, photocopying, recording, or otherwise, without the prior written permission of the author, except in the case of brief quotations in book reviews or scholarly works. For more information, contact the author at: www.talkpaperscissors.info/bravecreativehuman

Cover and text pages designed by Diana Varma
Edited by Mandy Bayrami

This book is dedicated to my parents and to my children; a foundation of self-esteem is the greatest gift I've ever received and it's the greatest gift I have to give.

This book is also dedicated to *the dreamers, the wishers, the liars, the hope-ers, pray-ers, and magic bean buyers*—thank you, Shel Silverstein, for the invitation.

May these pages be a whisper of enoughness in a noisy world demanding more.

Come in!
Come in!

CONTENTS

8   **Author's Note**
Before we begin

10   **Foreword**
By Guy Anabella, Drag Queen & Creativity Professor

INTRODUCTION

20   **Let's Begin**
Come one! Come all!

BRAVE

44   **Glass Half Full**
Technically, the glass is always half full, and it's also refillable

52   **You Are Not an Imposter**
You are a deeply-caring creative

66   **Making Friends with Failure**
Failure is part of the process, but it doesn't need to be part of our identity

84   Deciding on Enough
Enough is as good as a feast

CREATIVE

106   New Year x 3
September 1 + January 1 + May 1

114   Gutenberg's Social Media Presence
Haters gonna hate...but makers gonna make

122   Baking Pies
Same recipe, different ingredients

130   Mother Nature's Curriculum on Creative Practice
Spring has sprung and lessons are in full bloom

148   Certainty and Mysticism
Surrendering intellect to know the unknowable

158   Into the Deep
Glub, glub

HUMAN

170 **Less Strategy, More Humanity**
Create from the inside out, resisting the urge to create from the outside in

178 **The Opposite of Perfection**
is not imperfection

188 **Practice Makes Progress**
Less power-walking, more dancing

196 **Laugh Lines**
Changing the narrative, one story at a time

200 **Reflective Recalibration**
Running a 26.2-mile marathon requires a different pace than sprinting a 100-yard dash

212 ~~Restlessness~~
~~Dear Love, what will you~~
~~have me know today?~~

224 **No Map Required**
*May we follow the direction
of our creative compass*

236 **You Are Magical**
You are a brave creative human

GRATITUDE & NOTES

240 **A BIG Thank You**
It takes a village

244 **Notes**
Sources, sites, specifics

254 **Photo Credits**
Lending visuals to words

256 **About the Author**
Diana Varma, Curious Human

258 **Colophon**
*You can take the teacher out of
the classroom, but you can't take
the classroom out of the teacher...*

Author's Note

Before we begin

Hi, I'm Diana and I'm so glad you're here. Before I share my thoughts and ideas about brave creative humanity, I first want to share a note about my positionality. As a cisgender middle-class white woman, I am deeply aware that my perspective and life experiences are shaped by privilege. This privilege has afforded me opportunities and protections that are not universally shared, and I carry this awareness into my reflections on creative confidence. My understanding is imperfect and I am always learning. I invite you to engage with this book critically, to find connections where they exist, and to question where my perspective may fall short. My hope is that this book serves as a space where all readers can find gentle acceptance and belonging in their own creative confidence journey.

I am not a mental health professional, and the stories in this book are drawn from my personal experience. Nothing I share is intended as professional advice. If you are experiencing distress or navigating mental health challenges, I encourage you to seek support from a qualified professional. You are not alone, and help is available.

Foreword

*By Guy Anabella,
Drag Queen & Creativity Professor*

Drag artists of all kinds—queens, kings, and everything in between—embody the very essence of brave creative humans. We lip-sync, we dance, we design costumes, we master makeup—we use all that artistry to challenge societal norms and poke fun at gender stereotypes in the name of making the world a more inclusive, expressive, and vibrant place. It takes a whole lot of creative confidence to pull that off!

But I wasn't always this brave. Or creative.

It wasn't until I met the incredible Diana Varma—you might've heard of her—that I embraced my inner brave creative human.

A Story of a Brave Creative Human

The year is 2013 at Toronto Metropolitan University (formerly Ryerson University), and I was a tall, lanky guy in Diana's management class. There was something about her. I remember thinking, *she's kinda kooky, very smart, and super confident, and I kinda wanna be her.* At this time, I hadn't come out yet, and I certainly wouldn't have even considered doing drag. But something about Diana's powerful and creative feminine presence intrigued me.

About a month into class, I boldly (some might say brazenly) clunked myself to the front of the class 10 minutes before it started, and summoning confidence from somewhere, I blurted out, "I want to be your TA!"

She looked at me, straight-faced but kind, and said, "Okay. I'll let you know when the posting goes out."

I applied, got the role, and ended up being Diana's teaching assistant for my last year of undergrad and throughout my graduate degree. Over those three years, I learned a lot from her. Outside of class, we became really good friends, bonding over our shared interests—teaching, the '90s and 2000s, the art of drag, and how we could meaningfully contribute to this wild world in a positive way.

One spring day, Diana said, "I need you to cover a class for me. I'm going to a conference in Germany."

At the time, I had just completed my graduate degree and I had *zero* expectation of teaching anytime soon, especially at the postsecondary level. The class was starting in less than a week! Was I even ready? I felt like a damn imposter. But clearly, this lady saw something in me. She was more confident in me than I was in myself.

Anxious as heck, I said yes, because *hello*, what a wicked opportunity! And that's how I got my start teaching at the postsecondary level. I was well-received by students, and I realized that I truly loved teaching. Diana and I even ended up co-teaching a course together on creativity. It was a formative experience for me that I will always cherish.

As of writing this foreword, I have been teaching for almost a decade. I am now an award-winning creativity professor! My title is literally *Professor of Creativity* (how sickening is that?), and I owe my start to this fierce and fearless creativity queen who believed in me. Now I, too, get to help other humans be brave and creative. So cool, right?

The Birth of Guy Anabella

Oh, but sis—the story isn't done yet.

In 2019, I told Diana that I wanted to try drag just once. *Just once!* I figured I'd put on a show but never want to do it again.

One day, some friends and I went to Diana's house for a hangout. When we walked in, I saw some wigs lying on the table. At first, I thought they were *roadkill*—these wigs were cheap, but still cute. She said, "We're gonna do some light makeup and put the wigs on."

Diana did a long-ass eyeliner wing—probably about an inch long (*fierce!*)—some green eyeshadow, and a sassy red lip on me. No contour, no foundation, my mustache still stubbled out. But *girl*, when I tell you I *felt* my drag fantasy…*oh mama!!* Something from the drag heavens descended into my soul, and that was the night Guy Anabella was born.

Diana created that space for me. She was my drag mother. A drag mother (or parent) is someone who helps you start your drag journey—it's usually another drag artist. But in this case? It was unique because Diana doesn't do drag. Don't worry, though—we'll get her in drag soon. And when we do, she'll write a book about that too!

Fast forward again, and now I'm a *drag queen*—also known as the *brains, brawn, and beauty*. I'm a professor by day. I'm a powerlifter who can bench press 300 pounds because pretty girls are muscular, too. I represent my beautiful Guyanese culture through drag. I've performed in bars and on television, for crowds big and small. I've taught in drag and spoken at conferences in drag—the future looks bright. So much for wanting to try drag just once…(Look at what you started, Diana!)

I owe this, too, to Diana. She helped me see that both Chris (my name out of drag) and Guy Anabella are brave creative humans.

Why This Book? Why Diana?

So, all of this is to say that if you're looking to learn more about harnessing *your* creative confidence, Diana is most *definitely* your gal.

Now, let's be real…it's very unlikely that you'll get to be Diana's student, then her mentee-turned-bestie, and then her drag daughter (I mean, I won the lottery with that one). But you *do* have the next best thing—her book.

Diana has poured decades of experience, passion, and insight into this book. It is her gift to you: a labour of love and a testament to her lifelong dedication to teaching creativity and inspiring others. And now, it's in your hands.

Whether this book inspires you to become a fierce drag queen or just believe in yourself a little more, I *know* it's going to change your perspective.

In these pages, she breaks down the reframing *techniques, mindsets, and meaningful stories* that help people tap into their creativity and gain the confidence to express it. With her academic expertise, years of inspiring thousands of brave creative humans, and hands-on creative experience, Diana is the perfect person to guide you.

Diana's ideas in this book capture so much of what I've learned from her: creative confidence, showing up fully as yourself, and taking bold leaps even when you feel like an imposter. Whether it was stepping into a classroom for the first time as a professor or stepping into a wig for the first time as a drag queen, Diana taught me that creativity isn't just about skill, it's about courage. The lessons in these pages are the same ones she has instilled in her students, her colleagues, and her very grateful drag daughter.

And lucky you—now you get to learn from the best.

Lots of Love,
Guy Anabella ♡

Guy Anabella
Drag Artist & Creativity Professor

INTROD

UCTION

There is no better time to start than right now. Make something, build something, draw something, delight in something, be open to something…as the saying goes, "*these* are the good old days."

Let's Begin

Come one! Come all!

Let's begin with the most important, fundamental and transformative idea: **You are a brave creative human.**

Full stop.

You have an innate gift to think creative thoughts and make creative things, no matter how practical or frivolous. The world needs your ideas, creative energies, and unique points of view that only *you* can bring to life.

Whether you read this book from cover to cover, skim bits and pieces, or stop right here, it doesn't change the fact that you're *already* a brave creative human.

I'm so glad you're here to give yourself time to reflect on your brave creative humanity. We can all improve from wherever we're starting.

Sometimes we just need a gentle reminder that before society influenced us to judge our ideas as right or wrong—shaped by experiences in digital and physical spaces—our younger selves knew that the act of creating was exhilarating and fulfilling, no matter the outcome.

Let's get back to this place of inner knowing, creating from the truth that we are brave creative humans.

The Growth of an Idea

This book began as a collection of posts on the Substack platform under the name *The Creative Confidant*. It's a series about conjuring creative confidence, written and released story by story, created in a community space with a leaning towards experimentation.

Writing is something I've done more and more as my day job and passion projects have collided. I've written for industry magazines (long before I was ready), for university graduate degrees, for new online course developments, and for podcast episodes. The eight-year-old who never saw herself as a capable writer—especially next to her more articulate classmates—would be *shocked* to know that a big part of her grown-up job involves writing.

I like to think of my journey exploring creative confidence as scaling a tall beanstalk, its tendrils reaching into the clouds, initially planted as a tiny seedling in November 2021. During this time, I facilitated roundtable discussions about Gaining Confidence When You Don't *Feel* Confident at The Association of Registered Graphic Designers (RGD) Design reThinkers conference in 2021.

After the conference was over, I had a lingering feeling—an internal knowing—to continue exploring the topic with myself and with others.

I wrote an article based on my experiences called

"New Year, New-Found Confidence," which was published by the RGD in January 2022. It contains a series of ideas about changing one's perspective to find confidence in creative work, co-created with ideas from the 21 roundtable participants. The beanstalk was now as tall as my knees.

The article evolved into an invitation to speak at RGD's Creative Directions conference in 2022, where I joined participants to continue the important discussion, reframing the ideas holding us back. The beanstalk was now as tall as my waist.

Around the same time, I had the incredible opportunity to pitch a course idea to the team at Domestika, an online learning platform tailored for creatives. My creative intuition begged me to continue watering the beanstalk; it was now meeting my eyeline, as tall as ever. I flew to New York City to film the course with the Domestika team in the summer of 2022; and in January 2023, I was beyond grateful to share my first Domestika course with the world: *Building Creative Confidence: Unleash Your Potential.* With 2,000 students and counting, the beanstalk now stands taller than me, having grown much larger and faster than I expected.

From here, I've had the opportunity to continue speaking, teaching, and writing about failure, perfectionism, and imposter syndrome in creative work. You never know where an idea can lead!

After all, it could lead here, to writing a book.

The Creation of a Book, One Story at a Time

This big undertaking has been in the back of my mind for a while, and now feels like the right time and space to bring my ideas, stories, and invitations about creative confidence to the written page.

The process of writing a book is often described as a lonely and isolating undertaking, but I wanted the experience to be created in conversation with people around me. I aspired for these stories to be created in a space filled with community and focused on creative exploration, which is why releasing each piece of it along the way felt like the right fit.

My goal was to produce and publish a portion of the book each week. While I didn't stick to my original schedule (this collection took about 100 weeks instead of 20), it always felt good to put words to each story in my head, with the "Publish" button solidifying each story's existence in the world.

Thank you to everyone who accompanied me on this beanstalk adventure in real time and for those who are joining me now. May we keep our eyes to the skies, into the clouds of creativity.

Creative Confidence, Defined

There is no such thing as a 100% confident creative. I know I'm not and I bet you're not either.

Creative work wouldn't exist as we know it if there

There is no such thing as a 100% confident creative.

were people walking around with certainty during every step in their process. Creative exploration requires curiosity, trial and error, and even failure in the name of innovation. Certainty—in the process and in the result—simply isn't certain.

What's true is that your feelings of self-doubt are real. What's equally true is that it can be helpful to recognize and remove ideas that are no longer helpful to you.

Becoming more creatively confident isn't about changing yourself, but about changing your perspective so that you're not the one holding yourself back.

Let's start with a couple of definitions.

***Creativity can be defined as "the use of skill and imagination to produce something new or to produce art."*[1]**

It's helpful to separate creativity into two categories: creative thinking and creative making. Creativity is often associated with painters, musicians, and dancers, but scientists, mathematicians, and "left-brained" people of all kinds are incredibly creative too. Creativity is about problem solving. It's a state of mind—being open to possibilities and connecting existing dots, to create novel associations where they didn't exist before.

Maria Bowler, author of *Making Time: A New Vision for Crafting a Life beyond Productivity*, defines

Creativity is about problem solving. It's a state of mind—being open to possibilities and connecting existing dots, to create novel associations where they didn't exist before.

creativity as "cooperating with reality to draw out more life." She shares that "creativity reflects the fact that the life in you is in a reciprocal relationship with the life outside you."[2] Procedurally, creative thinking and making can be a collaborative act, solo act, or both. Experientially, creative thinking and making is never in isolation from the world around you.

One of the most exciting and hopeful parts about creativity is that it comes naturally to humans. We are born with the ability to be creative in our thinking. In my experience working with thousands of students, as well as in my own practice, creativity is much more "nurture" than it is "nature"; creativity is a muscle to be flexed and not born genius. As humans, we've been gifted the incredible ability to creatively solve problems, think abstractly, and wonder "but what if?"

Confidence can be defined as "a belief in your own ability to do things and be successful."[3]

One of my favourite anecdotes about confidence comes from clinical psychologist, Dr. Becky Kennedy: "To me, confidence isn't feeling like you're the best at something, it's feeling like it's okay to be you even when you're not the best at something. Confidence is really all about our relationship with our feelings[...]the most confident people, by the time they're adults, are just able to regulate the widest range of experiences."[4]

Confidence is such an interesting topic in the context

of creativity because it significantly influences our outputs, positively or negatively. For better or for worse, we often attach our identities to the work we put into the world, so negative reactions—while outside of our control—are often felt personally and deeply. This isn't a bad thing or a good thing…it's just a thing to be aware of and understand as it fuels the *why* of feeling confident. Awareness of shared understanding and affirmation that we're not the only one experiencing this feeling goes a long way to conjure our confidence as we engage creatively with the world.

Confidence, Meet Creativity

The areas that most impact our creative confidence are our passions, our people, our processes, and our patterns of thinking.

The *passions* we each have for a particular discipline, craft, or way of moving through the world are so important. It's these internally-fueled interests that help propel our motivations and keep us exploring. May we continue playing, no matter how silly our passions can sometimes look to the outside world. As long as they feel right to you, I urge you to keep tinkering.

The *people* in our lives shape how we perceive ourselves and influence our ability to stay curious and open to new ideas as we navigate life. As much as possible, surround yourself with people who support you and your creative practice. Even a single "creative confidant"—one person you can share your work with—can make all the difference in helping us live more creatively confident and connected lives.

The *processes* (or systems) in our days can help support creative practice or they can hinder it. A regular (or semi-regular) ritual of writing, making, and exploring helps to build our creative muscles and keep them from atrophying. Confidence develops through repetition, producing quantity, and is found in the *doing*. The more you can establish systems to stay in a creative practice—which means making time because finding time often means there will never *be* time—the more you will continue the positive, upward-looping feedback cycle where your creative confidence builds and reinforces over time.

The *patterns* of thinking we've been taught and sold are often not helpful to living an abundantly creative life. Being told that there can only be one winner, that the most senior decision makers are always right (e.g., teachers, coaches, bosses), that perfection is possible and even desirable in creative spaces, that work equals worth are all untrue and unhelpful in exploratory spaces. This is where I hope my book can help you as I share stories that have been at the heart of changing my own patterns of thinking about creative living.

What Creative Confidence is Not

Arrogance can sometimes be mistaken for confidence, which ironically, often stems from a *lack* of self-confidence and serves as overcompensation for self-doubt.

Creative confidence is also not:

- Being egotistical
- Being right all the time
- Being the loudest person in the room
- Establishing hierarchies of dominance over others
- Desiring greater control
- Being closed off to ideas

In fact, the most creatively confident people I meet walk through life choosing a path that is nearly opposite of the previous list. Instead, they embody attitudes and behaviours like:

- Celebrating other people's successes
- Openly admitting mistakes
- Deep listening
- Flattening hierarchies
- Embracing a loss of control to attune to the present
- Encouraging positive creative conflict

Furthermore, creative confidence is also being open to feedback. In fact, knowing that you *don't* have it all figured out and looking outside yourself for perspectives different from your own requires a great deal of self-confidence. Asking for feedback is a vulnerable act but it can create an upward spiral. Receiving feedback leads to improved understanding. Improved understanding leads to iteration. Iteration leads to deeper knowing—of yourself and of the world. Knowing leads to confidence. Rinse and repeat.

Infusing Creative Confidence into Models of Creativity

There are lots of creative thinking frameworks, but what I think virtually all of them are missing (even the most peer reviewed and accepted models) is the feeling of self-doubt. No matter who you are, where you are, or how much of an expert you are, if you're pursuing creative living, self-doubt (big or small) will present itself. If you're pushing into the unknown, failure will walk alongside you for at least some of the journey. If you're stepping outside of your comfort zone, you're stepping into territory where failure is likely—but so are novelty, surprise, delight, and innovation.

Let's take this popular cyclical creative process model that describes phases of creative ideation. The terms divergent and convergent are attributed to psychologist J.P. Guilford in 1956.[5]

If you're stepping outside of your comfort zone, you're stepping into territory where failure is likely—but so are novelty, surprise, delight, and innovation.

- **Diverge:** Many ideas are shared, often in a non-linear, free-flowing way.
- **Emerge:** New connections are formed based on the ideas generated.
- **Converge:** Ideas are organized and synthesized to produce a workable solution to be tested.

These models state steps in the process (the actions), but miss the underlying moments of self-doubt (the feelings) that creep in.

- **Diverge:** "This is a dumb idea."
- **Emerge:** "I have no idea how I'm going to connect all of these pieces."
- **Converge:** "Who am I to come up with a solution?! I don't know what I'm doing!"

I've certainly felt this way in the midst of a new project. I usually feel it more towards the end (the beginning is always the most exciting part for me), but I know others who feel this intensely at the start. The questioning, the wavering back and forth, and the uncertainty of it all...

And here's the interesting thing: becoming more creatively confident is not about removing moments of self-doubt, but anticipating them and using them as a catalyst for brave creative work that feels authentic to you.

More specifically, I choose to frame new creative pursuits as exciting rather than scary because I know that I am not only as good as my last idea or that

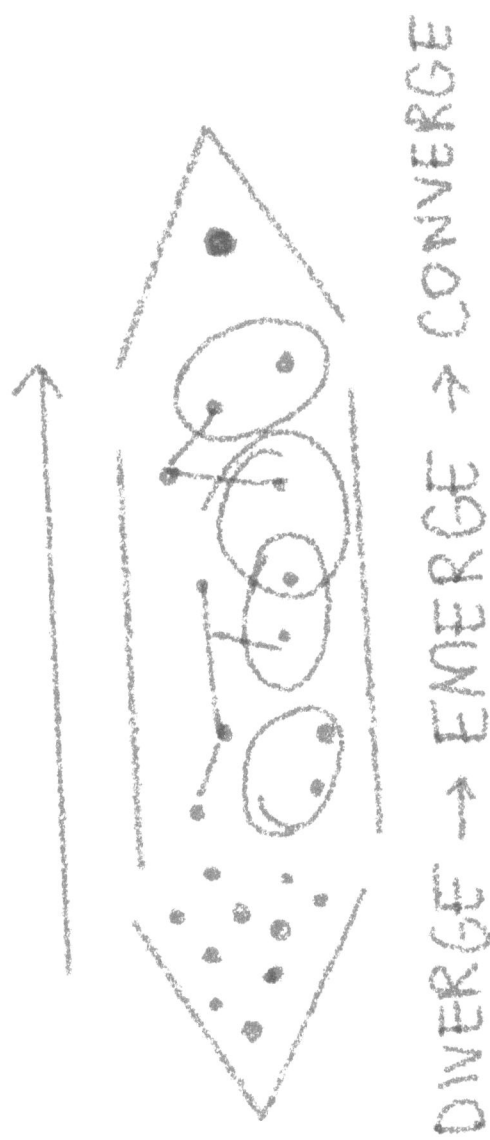

my worth is determined by my output. I have the self-awareness that finishing projects is hardest for me, particularly with projects I care deeply about. When I'm questioning the value my work brings to the world (like *right now*, making the final edits to this book!), I remind myself that this doesn't have to be the best or most important thing I ever create. I remind myself that the final product will be perfectly imperfect, sitting alongside all of the other perfectly imperfect work in the world. I know that walking alongside failure is what I've signed up for in creative work, that there's so much richness in the process of making, and that it's worth the risk.

- **Diverge:** "With quantity comes quality. I'll give myself the time and space to continue learning, iterating, and improving."
- **Emerge:** "I don't know where this is headed, but I'm capable of figuring things out as they happen, and I have the necessary grit to pick myself back up when they don't work out."
- **Converge:** "I'm not only as good as my last output. I might make mistakes, but I know I can handle it. Why *not* me?"

Instead of a finite, one-shot mentality, let's give ourselves permission to figure it out over and over again as we move through this messy creative process called life, pushing through self-doubt when it decides to join us along the way.

For years, I was missing an important link that I only recently realized: it's far less about the work I create and far more about the person I'm becoming through the act of creating, which you'll learn much more about in the following pages.

I'm So Glad You're Here

My goal is for this collection of stories to feel inclusive and accessible—something you want within arms reach when working on a new creative project. I will be vulnerable and honest, my words acting as both a trampoline (jumping off point) as well as a cushion (a soft place to land). I don't have all the answers, and my perspective is limited by my lived experience, but I hope these words feel familiar.

The book is divided into three sections: BRAVE, CREATIVE, and HUMAN, each containing stories that connect most closely with the section theme. This work is decidedly non-academic, derived from my personal views and experiences. Through this approach, I hope my written voice feels approachable, conversational, and familiar. With time and practice, my voice will be replaced with your own voice sharing similar confidence-boosting sentiments.

You will also find QR codes sprinkled throughout these pages. Some lead back to the website for this book to add visual context, while some are a little more suprising. I encourage you to interact with these digital nuggets, inspired by the experimental book-

making of the celebrated children's book author and memoirist, the late Amy Krouse Rosenthal.

If ideas in this book speak to you, please mark them up or underline them. Write down your own ideas in the margins around the text. There's no need to be careful or dainty with this book. The greatest compliment I can receive is for your copy to contain dog-eared pages, highlighted passages, and scribbled ideas.

May this be a resource that you can return to again and again as a companion for unapologetic, experimental, passion-fueled creative exploration.

Crayons as Creative Metaphor

I've always found great pleasure in opening a new box of crayons. As a child, I loved nothing more than a blank piece of paper and something to write with; no other toy could top this pocket-sized box of possibility. Very little has changed about my love for creative tools in the years since.

I've used my kids' art and their expressive strokes as inspiration for the connecting thread throughout this book's pages to unify individual stories. Crayons are a wonderful symbol for childhood creativity; an imperfect and versatile tool for expression used by children and inner children of all ages.

As celebrated educator Sir Ken Robinson stated in

his TED Talk, viewed more than 78 million times as of this writing: "I believe this passionately, that we don't grow into creativity, we grow out of it. Or rather, we get educated out of it."[6]

Let's get creative, colouring outside the lines and growing into ourselves in the process.

Will you join me?

Diana

Diana Varma
Curious Human

Doodle! Scribble! Draw!
Get creative on these pages.

I encourage you to be unprecious with this book, writing anywhere and everywhere.

Use this space to practice. :)

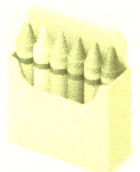

BRA

Get creative on these pages.

Here are some you-do-be-important with the blank.
writing an abroad anywhere.

Use this space to practice.

"Doing and making are acts of hope, and as that hope grows, we stop feeling overwhelmed by the troubles of the world." – Corita Kent[7]

Doing and making are concrete, ever-present ways to enact change—whether slow or swift, small or sizeable. Now is a good time to begin. To make something. To try something. To be a brave creative human.

Glass
Half
Full

Technically, the glass is always half full, and it's also refillable

You bring so much value to the world.

This bears repeating: You bring so much value to the world.

Not tomorrow, not when you learn a language, not when you finish a degree, not when you paint a masterpiece, not when you solve an important math problem, not when you write a #1 hit song, not someday.

You bring so much value to the world *today.*

I'm an optimist and this feels like an optimistic statement, but it's also a true statement.

As an optimist, if someone asked me, "Is the glass half-empty or half-full?" my predictable answer would be "Half-full!"

But isn't the glass *always* half full? If liquid makes up half the glass, then the other half must be filled with air. So technically, the glass is always full…

I want to show you that your glasses—the ones that represent the value you bring to the world—are already *so full.*

From Pitchers to Glasses and Back Again

When starting something for the first time, it's easy to let negative self-talk speak louder than our inner knowing, convincing us that we lack knowledge, skills, and experience to move forward with an idea.

To enter with brave energy, I've found that it helps to de-compartmentalize and compound everything I bring to a new situation. This expanded sense of self reminds me that I'm one of a kind and the only one to be able to do what I do, the way I do it. The same is true for you.

Imagine a pitcher of water sitting on a table alongside a row of empty drinking glasses. Each glass represents a part of your creative skill set: education, talents, interests, transferable skills, lived experiences, and lens through which you see the world. Imagine that water is poured from the pitcher into each glass, representing your capabilities in these areas.

For example, my first glass represents my formal education (from Kindergarten through to grad school), the next my technical skill set (different software applications I know inside and out), followed by my interests (storytelling, creative exploration) and transferable skills (project management, organization, creative problem solving).

It's easy to think of these glasses as individual silos with our glass for the new task ahead appearing empty, as if it's missing what we need to do, know, or bring. However, it's much more accurate and empowering to combine all of the water in the glasses back into the bigger pitcher (your whole creative self), appreciating the true value you bring. The individual glasses didn't need to be poured from the pitcher to begin with.

Pitchers and Podcasting

Podcasting was totally new to me a little over five years ago. I had zero experience with recording and editing audio, reaching out to guests, writing for audio, and publishing to podcast platforms.

While my glasses pertaining to these specific skills were definitely half empty, I had a wealth of glasses alongside the empty ones that were half full, some almost overflowing. I had years of transferable experience I brought with me in writing, sales, using design software, project coordination, and being a human who talks with other humans. Some of these I acquired in school or work settings and some through passion projects and my personal life, often through trial and error.

By mentally re-pouring the water from all glasses back into the pitcher, I felt a little braver. All experiences in my thirty-three years of life before starting my podcast helped me become a podcaster and produce episodes that could only be created by me, drawing from the collective contents of my unique pitcher of water and choosing to move into podcasting with brave, creative energy.

Bravery is a willingness to try—to not be good at something, but to give ourselves the breathing space and self-compassion to learn, grow, and evolve in the process. Bravery is acknowledging that we all bring so much value into this world, through a unique combination of life experiences.

This means that we're not starting from scratch with each new venture; we're starting from a wellspring of experience. And as we evolve throughout our lifetimes, we continue to fill our pitchers as we try new things. It reminds me of a quote by thought-leader Simon Sinek that resonates deeply with me: "People who wonder whether the glass is half empty or half full miss the point. The glass is refillable."[8]

Begin bravely, pitcher half full; continue with curiosity, refilling along the way.

Cheers!

Begin bravely, pitcher half full; continue with curiosity, refilling along the way.

When the orange crayon draws a sun for the first time, she feels a quiet confidence; a type of instinctive knowing that she's ready and capable. What she doesn't yet realize is that she carries yellow and red within her, colours she's blended a thousand times before.

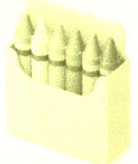

You Are Not an Imposter

You are a deeply-caring creative

A funny thing happened one Friday night before giving a talk about creative confidence. I was thinking about the presentation and procrastinating: "What do I *really* have to offer about this topic?"

On this particular Friday night, everyone in my house fell asleep early, and I felt like reading before bed. All of my books are in my eldest daughter's closet (also known as my *cloffice*, that I took possession of during the pandemic and never left) and even with the possibility of waking her, my gut told me to sneak in and grab a book. I didn't know what book, but I figured I'd decide when I got there. I tiptoed into the space, flashlight pointed at the floor, creaked open the closet door and stood in the dark scanning my bookshelf for inspiration.

Hmmmmmmmmmm…what book? I wondered, eyes navigating the colourful spines.

Just then, a little book called *The Practice: Shipping Creative Work* by Seth Godin caught my eye.

I'd started reading it years earlier but I hadn't picked it up since. I grabbed it, snuck back out of the room, and read.

And read.

And read.

And read.

And it's exactly what I needed in that moment:

"We allow others to live in our head, reminding us that we are imposters with no hope of making an original contribution. Our practice begins with the imperative that we embrace a different pattern, a pattern that offers no guarantees, requiring us to find a process and to trust ourselves."[9]

Okay, universe, you've got my attention!

And then, on page 28, Seth Godin, author of 19 international bestsellers who writes one of the most popular blogs in the world and is arguably the biggest thought leader in his discipline, said, "And I feel like an imposter often."[10]

You Share Because You Care

I love the way art therapist and author Amelia Knott reframes imposter syndrome. She insists that you don't feel imposter syndrome because you don't belong; rather it's a sign that you deeply care and want to deliver value in your work.

For me, this is where my imposter syndrome came from on the eve of that presentation—wanting to help those in the room through my experiences.

As I dug deeper into the topic of imposter syndrome, I learned that everyone, at all levels, feels imposter syndrome at least *sometimes*.

Here are four examples of the beautiful, the rich,

You share because you care.

the famous—those who appear to be living most confidently with it all figured out—feeling like imposters:

> *"So I have to admit even 12 years after graduation [from Harvard], I'm still insecure about my own worthiness...that every time I opened my mouth I would have to prove I wasn't just a dumb actress."* –Natalie Portman, Harvard Commencement (May 2015)[11]

> *"Writing is always full of self-doubt...by the time I wrote* Wild, *I was familiar with that feeling of doubt and self-loathing, so I just thought, 'Okay, this is how it feels to write a book.'"* –Cheryl Strayed, *Booth* (July 2014)[12]

> *"No matter what we've done, there comes a point where you think, 'How did I get here? When are they going to discover that I am, in fact, a fraud and take everything away from me?'"* –Tom Hanks, NPR (April 2016)[13]

> *"I go through [acute imposter syndrome] with every role. I think winning an Oscar may in fact have made it worse. Now that I've achieved this, what am I going to do next? What do I strive for? Then I remember that I didn't get into acting for the accolades, I got into it for the joy of telling stories."* –Lupita Nyong'o, *Time Out* (September 2016)[14]

What's at the core of imposter syndrome?

It's often rooted in *comparison.*

Comparison = Conformity and Competition

"Comparison is the crush of conformity from one side and competition from the other—it's trying to simultaneously fit in and stand out [...] Fit in, but win."[15] – Brené Brown, *Atlas of the Heart: Mapping Meaningful Connection and the Language of Human Experience*

How do we stop comparing ourselves to others so that we may feel less like imposters, and instead, feel the satisfaction that comes from living a creative life on our own terms?

The answer lies in removing the temptation to always compare.

In his book *Atomic Habits: Tiny Changes, Remarkable Results*, author James Clear shares that to break a bad habit, we must make it invisible. We must reduce our exposure and remove the cues of our bad habits from our environment. He shares the secret to self-control is simply that "...disciplined people are better at structuring their lives in a way that does not require heroic willpower and self-control. In other words, they spend less time in tempting situations."[16]

Social media—and the internet more broadly—has created a double-edged sword for creatives. Never before has it been easier to create and share work with an online audience, but it's also never been easier to see the work of so many talented people to which we can directly compare. Social media is a breeding ground for imposter syndrome; platforms built on the foundations of comparison, which can harbour discontent, dissatisfaction, and feelings that everyone's realities are far more exciting/successful/beautiful/intentional/better than our own. This can create a disconnect in the minds of creatives. The world is full of possibilities, but there's a sense of overwhelm, fear of failure, and a scarcity mindset that "it's already been done."

In search of rest over the 2021 winter break, I deleted Instagram for three weeks and I felt a weight lift that I didn't know I was carrying. I now delete the app on a regular basis when I feel the familiar pangs of imposter syndrome begin to creep in.

What are the other places and spaces that you know, deep down, are contributing to the imposter syndrome you may be feeling? How do you navigate removing the temptation of comparison from visual spaces on the internet if you are a creative business person who relies on these platforms to complete and promote your work? Because as Brené reminds us: "Comparison is a creativity killer, among other things."[17]

Reducing Temptation

It's not all or nothing. *Reducing* temptation is a softer, more accessible strategy than removing it entirely—especially when, as professional creatives, digital social platforms are used in various stages of the creative process.

To reduce temptation, be honest with yourself and commit to tucking away the apps (or downloading apps that will control this for you) contributing to your imposter syndrome so they're more difficult to access. Set boundaries around when and how long you spend in these digital spaces. The effort is real, but so is the lightness that comes from letting go of constant comparison.

Inspiration has existed in analog forms for thousands of years and it's readily available all around us. Instead of scrolling through Pinterest to develop a mood board, head to your local library or bookstore to browse beautiful books and magazines. Go for a walk and find inspiration in unlikely places, both natural and otherwise. Even an average walk through the grocery store may be the perfect place to find inspiration in beautiful packaging or to develop a new colour palette based on an exotic fruit. Some of the most interesting creative work comes from looking outside of the industry where we spend the majority of our time. When we find inspiration offline, we're far enough removed from the creators that direct comparison doesn't happen in the same way as it does online.

Better Work is Out There

Whether we compare ourselves to others often or infrequently, and whether we have harsh critics or unwavering cheerleaders, the fact remains that there will always be someone whose work seems "better" than ours (even though all creative work is subjective, and one person's masterpiece may be another's trash).

A reminder: *We are not our work.*

Separating ourselves from our work allows us to more objectively and openly acknowledge the truth in this statement, believing in our enoughness beyond the work we produce. Let's acknowledge that as creative people producing creative work, detachment can be difficult because our work reflects our personal identities, sensibilities, and ways of seeing the world. Feedback about our work is felt as feedback about us. And it's no wonder—educational systems conflate work and worth, particularly through traditional grading systems, beginning as early as when our age can be counted on a single hand.

But separating yourself from your work *can* be actively cultivated and practised.

It's simply a fact that someone will always have work that is more refined/professional/interesting/creative/noteworthy/special than ours. However, that doesn't mean that our work is any less important. "Better" in creative work is often subjective, contextual, and ultimately an unhelpful metric. Creative work is rarely binary—instead there are hundreds of different ways to approach a solution to a single problem. Our unique views, our life experiences, and our specific ways of thinking help us create work that is meaningful to ourselves and to others.

Furthermore, there can be upsides to seeing work that we deem better than ours. If we believe that we are not our work—uncoupling our identities from our outputs—it can be motivating to see others who have sustained long, creative careers. Seeing the growth in someone else's creative tenure can help us see our own evolution reflected in them. It gives us something to strive towards because creative living is a marathon, not a sprint.

Make a Ruckus

Imposter syndrome is often built on a rocky foundation of:

- External expectations
- Conditioned ideas of "right" and "wrong"
- Comparison to other people's successes without zooming out to see the big picture, including the backstage chaos to their onstage performance
- The mistaken notion that we are the work we produce

Imposter syndrome is real and I feel it at this very moment. I've found a volume dial on the all-too-familiar internal dialogue, and I can turn it down (even silence it!) with the right mindset and measures in place.

You are not an imposter. You are a deeply-caring creative doing important work for a world that needs your unique point of view and bold humanity.

As Seth implores us: "You have everything you need to make magic. You always have. Go make a ruckus."[18]

Creative work is rarely binary—instead there are hundreds of different ways to approach a solution to a single problem. Our unique views, our life experiences, and our specific ways of thinking help us create work that is meaningful to ourselves and to others.

Imagine if the indigo crayon never made its mark because it compared itself to the violet crayon. "I can never look like that."

What a loss this would be for indigo and the world.

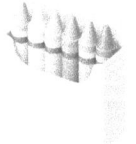

Making Friends with Failure

Failure is part of the process, but it doesn't need to be part of our identity

Have you ever found yourself watching an endless stream of ridiculous cat videos on YouTube while procrastinating from the important work you *should* be doing?

Yep, me too.

Why do we procrastinate? It's often because we're fearful. We're fearful of not knowing where to start. We're fearful of not knowing where we're going. We're fearful of not knowing how, where, or when to end.

We're fearful of FAILURE.

The humble Post-it note is an incredible creative tool. It should be acknowledged that the glue on the back of Post-it Notes was considered a failure when the idea was first conceived. According to 3M, the story goes something like this…

Dr. Spencer Silver, a 3M scientist, was trying to develop a stronger, stickier adhesive when he instead created the opposite: an adhesive that stuck lightly to surfaces and was able to be removed with ease. He failed, but he failed forward.

He believed that his idea had potential, but it wasn't until years later that he found the perfect use for his technology, when he collaborated with fellow 3M scientist Art Fry, who was frustrated by the bookmarked scraps of paper falling out of his hymn book.[19]

Around the same time, Fry remembered a seminar he'd attended about Dr. Silver's lightly sticky microsphere adhesion technology, finding a use-case for the "failed" invention.

And the rest—as they say—is history!

Let's Define Failure

A colleague shared with me that there's something emotionally powerful about defining something as "unsuccessful" (versus using the word "failure" outright) and he wondered how language shapes our experience of failure. The definition of failure is "lack of success" and "the omission of expected or required action."[20]

This is a beautiful opportunity to travel down a rabbit hole into the etymology of the word.

Failure (originally *failer*, 1640s) meant "a failing" or "deficiency," and came from the Anglo-French *failer* and Old French *falir*, meaning "to be lacking" or "to not succeed."[21]

I appreciate that both the definition and the origin of failure is referred to as the antithesis of success: "lack of success" or to "not succeed." If we can redefine success, we have the power to redefine failure.

If we can redefine success, we have the power to redefine failure.

Industrialist Economy vs. Connection Economy

Over the past century, our industrialist society has told us that success lies in conformity and compliance. In this model, success looks like climbing a predictable ladder to the top. It's hard to be okay with failure if we're taught that there's a right and a wrong answer, the former enabling a clear and linear path upward.

As Seth Godin describes in his book, *The Icarus Deception: How High Will You Fly?*, school has been transformed from a place of inquiry to a place of standards.[22] The industrialist age told us that there *are* answers and that you *need* them to succeed.

Seth believes that our industrialized systems have stripped students of their ability to innovate, express themselves, and take initiative. In essence, school has been un-teaching students how to acknowledge their authentic selves, instead encouraging them to rely on their conforming selves.

In the shifting age of our connection economy (represented by constant disruption, rapid innovation, and the democratization of tools), success looks different. Success belongs to those who are bold and creative and brave and connect and challenge the status quo.

Outputs vs. Inputs

Most examples of success are framed around outputs. Am I creating work that measures up to others? Am I creating work that is objectively "good?"

What if we reimagined success to not only reflect outputs, but also to include inputs? Curiosity, risk-taking, vulnerability, quantity of ideas (not *just* quality) and more?

While most traditional measures of success rely on outputs, we are not in control of our work once it leaves our hands. In contrast, measures of success that rely on inputs are within our control—our processes and feelings around those processes.

How might this shift the way we think about and define success in our own work?

Even still, there's something hugely vulnerable about the whole idea of producing creative work that might very well fail by standard measures of success.

How do we cope with the emotional realities of doing creative work that so deeply reflects our own identities?

How do we overcome the feelings of shame that can accompany something not going to plan?

How Do We Make Friends with Failure?

Making friends with Failure is a two-step process: the first step is to establish a healthy boundary with Failure and then—and only then—invite Failure to play.

For inspiration as to how we might get started, let's look to humans who bravely created things hundreds of years ago.

In her 2009 TED Talk,[23] author Elizabeth Gilbert shares the way that the people of Ancient Greece and Ancient Rome believed creativity to work. They believed that creativity was a divine spirit who visited human beings and gifted them with their creative ideas. As a result, they didn't believe that someone *was* a genius, but rather that they *had* a genius.

This helped them manage the emotional risk involved in creative work. After all, if they were wildly successful, they couldn't take all of the credit because their genius was at least partly involved.

If they were wildly unsuccessful—if they failed— they didn't have to take all of the blame because their genius was at least partially responsible.

What if success ("genius") and Failure are not two sides of the same coin, meaning only one or the other is possible? What if they are the *same* side of the same coin, with Failure being an integral part of success? What if Failure exists as part of the process but doesn't exist as a part of our identity?

Making friends with Failure is a two-step process: the first step is to establish a healthy boundary with Failure and then—and only then—invite Failure to play.

Sensing Failure

How do you sense Failure?

- What does Failure *feel* like?
- What does Failure *look* like?
- What does Failure *sound* like?
- What does Failure *smell* like?
- What does Failure *taste* like?

People I've asked have said that Failure looks like a shadowy figure lurking in the darkness, Failure sounds like nails on a chalkboard, Failure tastes metallic and off-putting.

Understanding how we each experience the sensations of Failure can help us recognize when it pays a visit, so we may reaffirm that it is separate from who we are as human beings. While Failure may choose to walk alongside us in our creative pursuits, *we are not Failure.*

If we can distinguish ourselves from Failure—acknowledging it as part of the process but not a fundamental part of our identity—we shed the weight of carrying our failures with us everywhere we go.

And what fills this newly-found space between ourselves and Failure? A world of opportunities, brimming with greater self-confidence.

But all of this makes Failure seem really bad. For all of the emotional turmoil that Failure causes, it's also misunderstood. Though often seen as an enemy at first, making friends with Failure can help us grow in unexpected ways.

What if we welcomed Failure with open arms, inviting it to play with us in our creative endeavours? Failure then becomes a co-creator, a confidant, a valued member of the team.

Let's Invite Failure to Play

1. Please grab a writing utensil and a piece of paper.
2. Using your dominant hand, simply write your name.
3. Consider how this feels. Is it easy? Comfortable? Familiar?

4. Switch hands and use your non-dominant hand to write your name.
5. How does this feel? Uncomfortable? Awkward? Clumsy? Great! A tiny experience of Failure.
6. Let's get weird! Please remove one shoe.
7. Place your pen or pencil between your toes and write your name. You will be bad at it. It will feel like Failure. But as we know, we are not Failure. We've invited it to play, so let's be good collaborators and welcome it into the process.

NOTE: If writing with your feet feels a little *too* weird, I encourage you to write your name with anything other than your hands. For example, you can place your pen in the crook of your elbow or in your mouth and try to write your name. The effect will be the same while keeping your feet planted firmly on the ground.

Making friends with Failure means that we're exploring uncharted territory, open to whatever is on the other side.

This will, undoubtedly, feel a little uncomfortable (not unlike what we just experienced). So how do we make it feel easier to fail?

I have three ideas:
- Break explorations into numerous small, low-stakes chunks, each offering the opportunity to succeed or fail, and then learn from either outcome.
- Do it more often. Because small chunks equal lower risk, get into the habit of inching outside of your comfort zone on a regular basis. If you make 100 tries, for example, you might succeed 40, 50, 60, 70, 80 or more times. That's HUGE—and far more wins than if you had never tried at all (and think of all the figuring out along the way!).
- If the word "failure" still feels unsettling, feel free to use "surprise" or "data" instead. May this new word choice remind you of all the

possible greatness that can come from your experimentation.

The act of failure can help us understand ourselves and the world around us far better than if we'd never experienced it.

Failure helps drive innovation forward in ways that getting it right every time will never allow.

Failure separates us from the machines.

Failure makes us human.

Get curious, experiment, try, do, surprise, fail, observe, acknowledge, embrace, learn, grow—then do it all over again. This is what happens when we make friends with Failure, redefining success in the process.

Much like the un-sticky Post-it Note glue, you never know when experimentation that initially seems like a failed attempt can spark a whole new direction of inquiry and change the world in the process.

Everyday Failures

I'm so grateful to the many incredible people helping to normalize Failure. For example, author Brad Montague (*The Enthusiast* and *Becoming Better Grownups*) holds Fail-a-brations to celebrate moments of failure and what we've learned from them.

It's when we can acknowledge Failure as a community that we can collectively unravel our complex conditioning with success, unlearning that we're only as good as our outputs.

Improv artists fail all the time and do it so beautifully. Their entire process is about vulnerability, trying, receiving feedback, and "failing forward" into the next show. Night after night after night.

It's when we can acknowledge Failure as a community that we can collectively unravel our complex conditioning with success, unlearning that we're only as good as our outputs.

We can begin to uncouple work and worth.

The Cat Came Back

I'd like to end this section by sharing one final story of failure in the digital media realm: YouTube. Originally conceptualized as an internet dating site, with the tagline "tune in, hook up," YouTube's founders had a very different vision of the platform. As detailed in his 2007 convocation speech[24] (found on YouTube, naturally), one of the founders, Jawed Karim, shared this initial vision for the pioneering website.

After five days and not a single singles video uploaded to the site, the founders took to Craigslist and offered to pay women $20 to create and upload a video (...and they didn't get a single reply). Still, the founders believed that their video sharing idea had potential. So, while they initially faced failure, they stuck with it and pivoted to create one of the most popular websites on the internet that experts say has shifted society into a "moving video culture."[25]

And without YouTube, we wouldn't have so many ridiculous cat videos to watch while procrastinating out of fear of failure.

And, hey, maybe we can learn from these cats. We can appreciate their unapologetic curiosity—their desire to experiment, to try, to make the jump even if failure is a possibility…

And sometimes, you just go for it and magic happens. Like when a cat takes a (literal) leap of faith and happens to land *precisely* in the right spot.

Go forth and make friends with Failure!

The crayon coloured and coloured and coloured so hard that it snapped. Broken into two pieces, it thought, "I failed. That's it..."

"But wait!" it said. "I can do *twice* the colouring now!"

Broken crayons still colour.

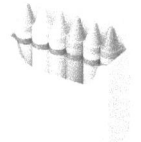

Deciding on Enough

Enough is as good as a feast

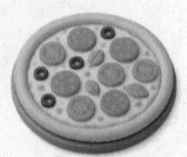

I recently fell into a social media comparison trap with a content creator I've followed for a long time. I fell fast, tumbling down the "what if" rabbit hole before I even realized it was happening.

This creator is a very successful female creative business owner who is around my age and also has two little girls. A recent video she posted stopped me in my tracks, my comparison engines revving at full speed as the short video montage played. It featured her and her husband with their newborn baby daughter, happy together in the hospital. Text overlaid the video, showing the passive income her business generated on the day she gave birth.

It wasn't a small number.

Doing a quick calculation (and all things being equal) her passive income streams generate roughly $2.5 million in revenue each year.

Whoa.

The whole point of the post was to promote the ways in which email marketing has allowed her business to grow at an exponential rate, the caption reading: "If your business is reliant on you showing up, you don't have a business…you have a job."

My mind immediately went into strategy mode:
- How can I replicate this success?
- How can I be making passive income at even a fraction of what she earns?

- How can I replace my "job" with a "business"?
- How do I do what I'm doing but bigger? Better?!

Before I continue, I want to say that I genuinely respect this individual, and I think what she puts into the world is both meaningful and marketable, but the information she shared that day sat like a lump in my gut.

With dissatisfaction for my life and my work and my worth beginning to brew, I stopped myself and I got still. What was I feeling?

Was it desire? Was it longing? Was it jealousy?

Surprisingly, it wasn't any of the above.

After contemplation (paired with a heavy dose of gratitude, reflecting on the abundance in my life), I realized what I was feeling in that moment was simply a need to hear a different perspective, a different story. A story of enoughness in a world constantly demanding more.

And it became clear that I needed to do some research and write this narrative for myself and for anyone else who would benefit from hearing it, so I hope the following words encourage you to decide what's enough for yourself, while recognizing that more is not always better and celebrating that there are many (many!) different approaches to solving the same problem.

Enough is Enough

When I'm grappling with a tough issue, I find that it helps to tap into my tried and tested toolbox containing my telescope, microscope, stethoscope, and kaleidoscope.

Telescope

My telescope allows me to zoom out and see the big picture. It helps me realize that I've grown compared to who I was two years ago, two months ago, and even two weeks ago. My telescope helps me better understand that very few things thrust upon me are truly urgent, allowing me to respond appropriately and in due time.

What are my needs and what are my wants, both financially and creatively? How much money do I need to support my family and how can I earn it without having to make a major course correction in my career?

I am incredibly privileged to be able to do work I enjoy that provides a liveable income. There will always be aspects of my job that I'd rather avoid, but I get paid to do work I believe in—work that puts a roof over my head, food on the table, and leaves some left over for non-essentials. I often think about the few years I spent after graduating from university, living in my grandparents 1950s bungalow just north of Toronto. Each of the closets in the three bedrooms are very small by today's standards. My grandparents' post-WWII generation was not immersed in the same level of highly-targeted mass consumerism as we are today, so they didn't need huge closets. The equivalent closet in my current home is easily 5 to 10 times more space...and it's *full*! The omnipresent and targeted nature of today's advertising is hugely influential in shaping our society's consumer behaviour. And I don't think I'm objectively any happier than my grandparents because of this stuff, so why on Earth would I need or want any more than I already have?

Income inequality is significant both locally and globally. According to Credit Suisse's 2018 Global Wealth Report, a net worth of just over $90,000 USD (assets minus debts) means you're still richer than 90% of the people on Earth.[26] Furthermore, if you have just over $4,000 you're richer than 50% of the world's population. The amount of money needed to live is very much dependent on your geographic location—countries and cities vary widely—but the discontent I was feeling made me really think about what enough money looked like for me. Which brings me to another key question...

Why would I aspire to build a business that generates $2.5 million a year?

This sounds like a ridiculous question (I mean who wouldn't want $2.5 million rolling into their bank account each year?!), but I seriously have to ask myself why I need this much money. Because it would require spending time and energy growing my following, serious list-building, and working on the business side of creativity to promote myself in a way that I'm just not interested in doing for a huge sum of money—more than I would ever need.

After all, extreme wealth is an experience in this life. Once needs are met and financial security is found, money is not life-changing. To quote actor Jim Carrey: "Alrighty then!" Just kidding, he said this: "I wish everyone could get rich and famous and everything they ever dreamed of so they can see that's not the answer."[27]

In a 1978 study entitled "Lottery Winners and Accident Victims: Is Happiness Relative?" researchers compared happiness levels of 22 major lottery winners, 22 control participants, and 29 paralyzed accident victims. The study found that the lottery winners were not as happy as you'd expect, and the accident victims were not as unhappy as you'd expect.

The results of the study noted that "Eventually, the thrill of winning the lottery will itself wear off. If all things are judged by the extent to which they depart from a baseline of past experience, gradually even the most positive events will cease to have impact as they themselves are absorbed into the new baseline against which further events are judged. Thus, as lottery winners become accustomed to the additional pleasures made possible by their new wealth, these pleasures should be experienced as less intense and should no longer contribute very much to their general level of happiness."[28]

Hedonic adaptation—the tendency to get used to new things with dissipating happiness, constantly creating new baselines—is both a blessing and a curse. A blessing in the face of tragedy and a curse in the face of successive levels of happiness. Everything is relative, and while more money will provide short-term thrills, 50 years of psychological study shows us that it won't provide long-term, lasting happiness.

Microscope

My microscope allows me to zoom in and pay attention to the details, appreciating the small, everyday wonders available to me if I'm looking for them.

What do I look forward to each day? What gets me up in the morning?

In their book *Ikigai: The Japanese Secret to a Long and Happy Life*,[29] authors Francesc Miralles and Héctor García interviewed more than a hundred elderly residents of Okinawa, Japan (a Blue Zone with some of the longest life expectancies in the world) to discover commonalities that helped many live long, healthy lives. Beyond a healthy diet and physical activity, they found that Okinawans have something unique in each of their lives that they feel is worth living for. *Ikigai* refers to a passion that gives value and joy to life. In approaching each day with an ikigai in mind, finding joy and purpose is not about needing to eradicate work, but doing meaningful work with and for meaningful people.

Aside from spending time with my family and my dog taking me out for walks, what gets me up in the morning is writing, reading, dreaming up new ways to build community in my classroom, developing creative prompts for students, finding new interesting people with whom to have interesting conversations about design, making, and teaching.

Stethoscope

My stethoscope allows me to hear—really listen—to myself, the world around me, and the people in it. There are few gifts as coveted and as rare as someone giving us their full attention. (This particular scope wasn't always in my toolbox, but my brilliantly creative and insightful friend, Nat Lumby, suggested I add this one, as well as the next.)

If I listen deeply to what my inner knowing is trying to tell me, what I hear is…

A passive income makes so much sense. By putting in hard work and effort now, I can save time and produce huge results in the future.

But if I listen a little more deeply, what I hear is actually a question…

Can I do more with less?

If I'm doing meaningful work for meaningful people that pays the bills, is there really a need to change that? To fix something that isn't broken? Can I make my needs fewer so that I may live more richly and more satisfied with what I have instead of constantly longing for excess?

After all, money is a two-sided equation: income and spending.

And the rules of the equation are simple: spend less than you make and save some for later.

This is a common thread in the minimalist community. You don't need a lot of money to live a beautiful life. You don't need fancy things to live a beautiful life. Cultivating strong relationships will make you far happier than stuff ever will.

In fact, Harvard conducted the longest-ever study on happiness (THE HARVARD STUDY OF ADULT DEVELOPMENT[30]) that began in 1938 and lasted 85 years with hundreds of global participants who were studied in an effort to discover what makes humans happy. Researchers found that career achievement, money, exercise, and a healthy diet were not the foremost happiness predictors. Instead, positive relationships were consistently found to make us happier, healthier, and live longer. If you're looking for a long-term investment that's most proven to pay (metaphorical) dividends, community and connection are sure bets. Money can buy you necessities and comfort, but it can't buy you happiness.

Money can buy you necessities and comfort, but it can't buy you happiness.

This has me thinking about Maslow's Hierarchy of Needs, a pyramid of physiological and psychological needs said to motivate human action in ascending order: life-sustaining needs like food and water; safety and security; social needs like friendship and family groups; and, finally, self-esteem and self-actualization/personal growth at the top.

Financial blogger Mr. Money Mustache observes the backwards nature of trying to buy happiness: "Our consumer culture encourages us to look upwards and earn respect, sexual intimacy, confidence, and even self actualization with the new Toyota Highlander or Ford F-150, when doing so actually destroys our security."[31] It's almost like we're trying to flip the pyramid on its head and it feels impossible to find balance in this precarious upside-down state.

Instead of longing for more and building a business that can afford all the luxuries of the world, what if I can do more with less?

Kaleidoscope

My kaleidoscope allows me to appreciate joy, experience play, and feel child-like wonder as I move through this short, precious, mysterious life.

When it comes to work, I have an audacious, countercultural, and unrealistic-sounding goal: work needs to be a source of fun. I actively prioritize joy, experimentation, and play in my classroom. From an outsider's perspective, it may appear trivial or unimportant to approach work in this way, but a light-hearted approach to rigorous work makes all the difference for my students and me. Creative prompts, Crayola markers, and curiosity greet us at the start of each class. "Serious fun" helps students connect to the material inside and outside of the classroom, as well as connect students to themselves, their peers, and to me as their instructor.

If I can sustain myself and my family doing work that I genuinely enjoy, why would there be any need to make more money doing work that I objectively enjoy less?

This reminds me of the fable of *The Fisherman and the Businessman*[32], shared in many books and publications and translated into English by author Paulo Coelho. It's the story of a businessman who visits a small Brazilian village and strikes up a conversation with a fisherman who enjoys a leisurely life of catching fish, playing with his kids, taking an afternoon nap, and having a drink with friends in the evening. As the conversation progresses, the businessman tries his best to convince the fisherman to scale up his business—catch more fish, invest in better equipment, and build a thriving enterprise—so that one day he may be successful and live a leisurely life of catching fish, playing with his kids, taking an afternoon nap, and having a drink with friends in the evening. But, of course, the fisherman is already living the life the businessman promises in the distant, long-term future.

I am privileged to have fun spending my days teaching, making, and talking to interesting people about interesting things. If I desire to become wealthy beyond my wildest dreams, I can actively build a business through intense self-promotion, clever email marketing, and other spelled-out strategies used by traditionally-successful content creators. Once I expend great energy, time, and resources getting to a point where I could have almost anything I could ever desire, I can then begin to do what I really want: spend my days teaching, making, and talking to interesting people about interesting things.

Slaying the Enoughasaurus

One of the many thought-provoking people whose journey I follow is Annie, a minimalist living in Los Angeles, the land of fame, fortune, and excess. She enjoys simple pleasures and helping others see her countercultural perspective on doing more with less.

One day she shared a simple and profound phrase that practically leapt off the screen at me: **enough is a decision, not a number.**

I took a screenshot, which I've revisited many times since. Before that moment, I had never thought about enough being a decision; something I could choose for myself, something entirely within my control.

I've learned that thinking about enough as a number simply doesn't work. There's always the next best thing out there to tempt us. Do I like nice stuff? Sure. Am I enticed by beautiful clothes and fun gadgets? All the time.

But when I choose to adopt the mindset that enough is a decision and not a number, I can stop trying to accumulate more in an attempt to buy happiness. That dress *I couldn't live without* now sits alongside all of the other clothes in my closet. And it doesn't have nearly the same appeal now that I own it, underscoring the reality that the anticipation leading up to acquiring something is often more fulfilling than owning the item itself. Not to mention the added costs of maintaining, storing, and ultimately discarding the item, along with the emotional guilt of not getting my money's worth and the clutter that comes with acquiring more and more and more…

As author of *The Cheapskate Next Door*, Jeff Yeager, puts it: "Conditioning yourself to spend less and to be content doing so is the way to slay your Enoughasaurus […] At what point of accumulating more things can you be content?"[33]

Financial author Dave Ramsay puts it another way: "We buy things we don't need with money we don't have to impress people we don't like."[34]

Buying the latest and greatest to *keep up with the Joneses* is flawed…the Joneses are broke! Household debt in North America continues to rise at staggering

Enough is a decision, not a number.

rates ($16.9 trillion in the fourth quarter of 2022!), due to higher mortgage, auto, and student loan balances, according to the Federal Reserve Bank of New York.[35]

All things considered (and we haven't even touched on the devastating environmental impacts of conspicuous consumption), I choose to make the decision that I have enough. My stuff does not define me, no matter how convincingly targeted ads try to tell me otherwise.

My best friends will not stand up at my funeral and say, "She had really nice clothes and her shoe collection was incredible!" My best friends will hopefully talk about my kind heart and my generous spirit and all the other qualities that make me *me*.

This doesn't mean I won't ever yearn for new stuff or buy things I don't need (hello, new hammock), but I ultimately have the final say, and not the other way around.

Enough is a decision. I decide that I not only have enough, I have more than enough. I *am* enough.

Fortune(ate) Cookies

Circling back to where we began, I respect and applaud the content creator making this strategy work for her, finding massive monetary success along the way. However, it's not necessary for me to pursue the same path, feeling less than for my differences in time, influence, and income. It's just not a good match.

My telescope, microscope, stethoscope, and kaleidoscope have helped my strategically-minded gut feel more settled, guiding me back to my different—yet equally abundant—path. A path of creative exploration interwoven into a teaching job and infused with a huge dose of gratitude throughout. I've found meaningful work with and for meaningful people, and I have a community where I can foster new connections, investing in current and future happiness.

More money/stuff/power/influence isn't always better. Sometimes the answer can be found in doing more with less; addition by subtraction.

As a fortune cookie I opened once read: "Enough is as good as a feast."

And I feel full.

Why settle for a box of eight crayons when you could have 24, 64, or even 96?

More crayons mean more possibilities—new shades, richer details, bigger ideas!

But abundance isn't just about having more—it's about knowing how to work with what you have. The leap from zero to eight crayons is transformative, opening a world of colour where none existed before. From eight to 96, the range expands, but not critically so. In fact, a smaller set can offer focus, ease, and proficiency in a world that insists that more is always better. True creativity isn't about how many crayons you have—it's about what you do with what you have.

CREA

I recently watched Kermit the Frog give the 2025 commencement address at the University of Maryland's graduation ceremony. In a whimsical 11-minute speech, where he was donned in a Kermit-sized cap and gown, he emphasized the importance of connection and dreaming big.

"Be a Kermit the Frog. Have a creative vision and no ego. Recognize the unique talents of those around you. Attract weirdos. Manage chaos. Show kindness. Be sincere."[36] – @timescanner

What a brave creative amphibian.

New Year x 3

September 1 + January 1 + May 1

In my brain and body, the new year comes not once, not twice, but three times each 365 days. I feel lucky that I have the chance to pause and reflect on my creativity multiple times each year.

September 1: New Year #1

The first new year happens as the calendar rolls from August to September, marking the end of the summer holidays and the start of the new school year.

Like all students, I've experienced the cyclical nature of school for decades. This is one of my very favourite things about still operating in a school environment; the finite and partitioned nature of the work. There's a clear beginning, middle, and end—something my world sorely lacked in a traditional 9-5 environment.

September always feels like a new beginning, where I can choose any new path that lies ahead, feeling a renewed sense of vigour for the inevitable challenges.

I liken this September new year to that of a caterpillar, crawling along with a sense of hope and purpose. I can focus on consuming and applying knowledge to new scenarios and relationships along the journey. There is a hungry energy to this new year; an insatiable desire to move forward with speed and tenacity, knowing that there is a time limit on this phase before moving to the next.

January 1: New Year #2

This time of year is punctuated by neatly tucked away Christmas decorations and freshly-vacuumed floors, as well as bare walls and surfaces that feel luxurious in their sparseness. The week between Christmas and the start of the new calendar year always feels like a bridge; a liminal space from one big annual milestone to another, squeezed into a tiny timeframe.

Yet, it's this timelessness—both stretched and hurried, short and long—that makes the arrival of the new year a perfect moment to reflect and reset. The lead up to the new year feels ripe with possibility and hopefulness for what's to come.

My very favourite annual ritual is to create a visual/mood board to capture my hopes and ideas for the next several hundred days. Each year this becomes a visual representation of my forward-oriented ideas, as well as an opportunity to look back on visuals from past years that give me a glimpse into my growth and frame of mind year-over-year.

I liken this January new year to that of a chrysalis. January and the following winter months naturally feel like a time to ebb more than flow, taking a nod from the bears and frogs and trees that hunker down during the colder, darker winter months. This is not so much a stopping, as it is a slowing down; it's a time to be extra intentional about choices today that will make the biggest difference tomorrow.

May 1: New Year #3

Where I live in the world, early May is the time when nature is slowly awakening from its months-long slumber, opening its eyes slowly with a deep remembering sinking into its roots. Nature gets its bearings and then leaps enthusiastically out of bed in an array of colours and blooms in a transformation unlike any other.

This time of year feels as though Mother Nature has been holding her breath, ready for the right time to exhale. It's a spectacularly hopeful time with a sensory overload of sights, sounds, and smells. The cherry blossom tree above my mailbox delivers the most beautifully powerful, intoxicating scent I've ever experienced. The hostas grow so quickly, I could sit and watch them transform in real time. And the people (the people!) triumphantly walk out of their front doors to enjoy the warm spring air and glorious sunshine we've all forgotten feels so good.

I liken this May new year to that of a butterfly. This new year—more than any other—feels like the most fully-realized emergence that is wholly different from the others. It's an awakening to the magic of the Earth and a reminder of the absolute living miracle of life on this planet.

It's a reminder that human-centred ways of living—including the many destructive systems that humans have erected—are immature, toddler-like, broken understandings of our world that pale in comparison to the mature reality that all living beings can exist in alignment on this planet.

Each of the three new years brings hopeful energy relative to its time and stage; exactly *what* it needs to be *when* it needs to be.

Happy new years, from my chrysalis to yours.

Each of the three new years brings hopeful energy relative to its time and stage; exactly *what* it needs to be *when* it needs to be.

For months, my kids kept crayons tucked away in a pencil case in our car, always ready for inspiration to strike between destinations. But day after day, night after night, these crayons remained untouched, until one fall afternoon when the kids went searching for them.

Instead of tall, intact crayons, they found swirling, contorted masses of wax, melted by summer's heat and reshaped by time and circumstance.

"wowwww!" they gasped from the back seat.

"neat!" I exclaimed from the front.

A bit of alchemy, a bit of science, a bit of magic. What could have been interpreted as ruined was, in fact, transformed—a reminder that new beginnings often take unexpected shapes.

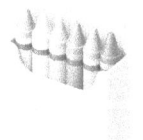

Gutenberg's Social Media Presence

*Haters gonna hate...
but makers gonna make*

Imagine if Instagram had been around 550+ years ago when Johannes Gutenberg was making brave creative work, printing the first commercially-viable book in Europe that would set off a global movement and pave the way for a world shaped by the sharing of information.

On the following page is what Gutenberg's Instagram account may have looked like.

Even the most incredible people doing the most incredible work of their time had haters. In this case, Gutenberg wasn't liked by scribes who were handwriting manuscripts at a much slower pace than what was possible on a printing press. They felt threatened by his technology, seeing the writing on the wall that their jobs would soon be radically changed because of this creative work.

Let's acknowledge three hard truths:

1. Not everyone is going to appreciate what you're doing or making.
2. Not everyone is going to understand your creative journey.
3. Not everyone is going to like you.

While this can be a hard pill to swallow (especially for the people pleasers among us!), this is *not* a good enough reason *not* to live a bold, authentic, creative life.

This may even mean that you're onto something.

gutenberg_books

Today's the day, dear followers! I've made it happen. I've taken moveable type, my converted wine press and printed the first page of what's to become 1286 pages of greatness! Order your copy today! (Link in bio)

scribe_guy1423 Who do you think you are? This is the most inauthentic work I've seen in a while. No one is going to buy a book that's NOT crafted by hand. You're a fraud!

illuminator_max I can't wait for this! You're a genius doing so much greatness. The world needs your work!

handwriting4life booo you suck

However, in the age of digital everything, the ability to read the thought trails of others—almost in real time—can be a powerful demotivator. I've seen incredible creative works posted on social media and genuinely thought: "Wow! This person is doing amazing things." But all it takes is one look at the comments to find someone who has said something negative. It doesn't take long to find polarizing views, snap judgements, and hurtful remarks to brave creative work shared online.

By contrast, Gutenberg was able to print copies of his typeset Bible without the ever-present backlash, disapproval, and skepticism of others at his fingertips.

Imagine if Gutenberg put his feet up after a long day and doom-scrolled Instagram before bed, only to be met with a barrage of negative backlash about his work. How might that have changed his process or his willingness to try and put his creation out there? Perhaps he would have scaled back or stopped printing altogether. In an ironic twist, social media as we know it today might not have been possible if it had existed 550+ years ago, stopping great makers before they ever got started.

While social communication platforms aren't going anywhere anytime soon, does the pressure of performing in these digital spaces mean we should stop creating—doing so confidently, with gumption and bravery?

Of course not.

As Amie McNee, author of *We Need Your Art: Stop F*cking Around and Make Something*, explains: "When you share your art, she starts doing work for you [...] Your art leads a secret private life, she doesn't tell you about all that she's doing. But she's talking to people, getting stuck in people's heads, changing lives on the sly."[37]

In the process of living brave creative lives we must keep moving forward, following our creative intuition, which often holds multiple truths: it's foreign, yet familiar; elusive but ever-present; terrifying and exciting. It's knowing you're onto something, often without fully understanding what that *something* will become.

Perhaps disagreement, objection, and skepticism from the masses is even a *cornerstone* of truly brave creative work because following your creative intuition means that not everyone will get it.

Just like Gutenberg, your next great idea has the potential to change the world.

Haters gonna hate…but makers gonna make.

Keep making.

Perhaps disagreement, objection, skepticism from the masses is even a *cornerstone* of truly brave creative work because following your creative intuition means that not everyone will get it.

Perhaps
disagreement,
objection, skepticism
from the masses is
even a cornerstone
of truly brave
creative work
because following
your creative
intuition means
that not everyone
will get it.

A squiggle, a scribble, a mark that feels good. Colour outside of the lines. It doesn't have to make any sense to anyone else if it feels like important creative work to you.

Baking Pies

*Same recipe,
different ingredients*

My aunt is a fabulous baker. Cookies, cakes, sweet breads, squares. They are all so delicious, but my absolute favourite is her gingerbread cookies. They are unlike the hard, cakey store bought gingerbread; they are thin and soft and melt in your mouth with a perfect amount of royal icing on top. I have to admit that when my aunt's baking comes out at family gatherings, I reach for those gingerbread cookies like my life depends on it. ("Grownups first! Sorry kids!") After all, there's only so much to go around.

A scarcity mentality is a belief that there are a finite number of resources, roles, or creative outputs in the world and that once they're used up, there's no space for any more.

Scarcity mentality can become an excuse that has us second guessing our creative confidence: "There's already someone out there who's doing what I want to do; they got there first so there's no room for me."

It's as though you've missed the opportunity to find your slice of the pie. That pie definitely *looks* complete. So what's an aspiring creative to do?

Why not bake another pie?!

Goodness knows that there's lots of gingerbread cookies in the world, but that doesn't stop my aunt from making more all the time. There are likely hundreds or even thousands of variations of the classic gingerbread cookie recipe, each delicious and valid—a sensory celebration in its own right.

The fact that others are already doing what you want to do is not a good enough reason *not* to do it.

Do it for the joy in the journey.

Do it for the creative expression and expansion it brings.

Do it because it feels good to do it.

Do it because you can't *not* do it.

If you want to be a landscape artist who designs French gardens, do it. If you want to be a writer and craft an adventure novel about eating your way across the country, do it. If you want to design a beautiful typeface in a sea of beautiful typefaces, JUST DO IT.

Let's give ourselves and others permission to create in meaningful ways even if it seems like others are doing the same thing.

By engaging in work that feels authentic to each of us, there will always be room for everyone to pursue their calling. There's room for everyone and their pies—and their gingerbread cookies, and their paintings, and their dances, and their writing, and their music, and their art.

In the words of the beautiful Alok Vaid-Menon, "Authenticity is not a destination, it's an orientation and what matters more is that you're showing up, not where you're going."[38]

The creative outputs you bring forth will never be

exactly the same as the creative outputs of another. After all, you're creating from the same recipe, but using different ingredients—your unique combination of ingredients—that are deliciously unique to you.

Keep showing up. Keep baking pies.

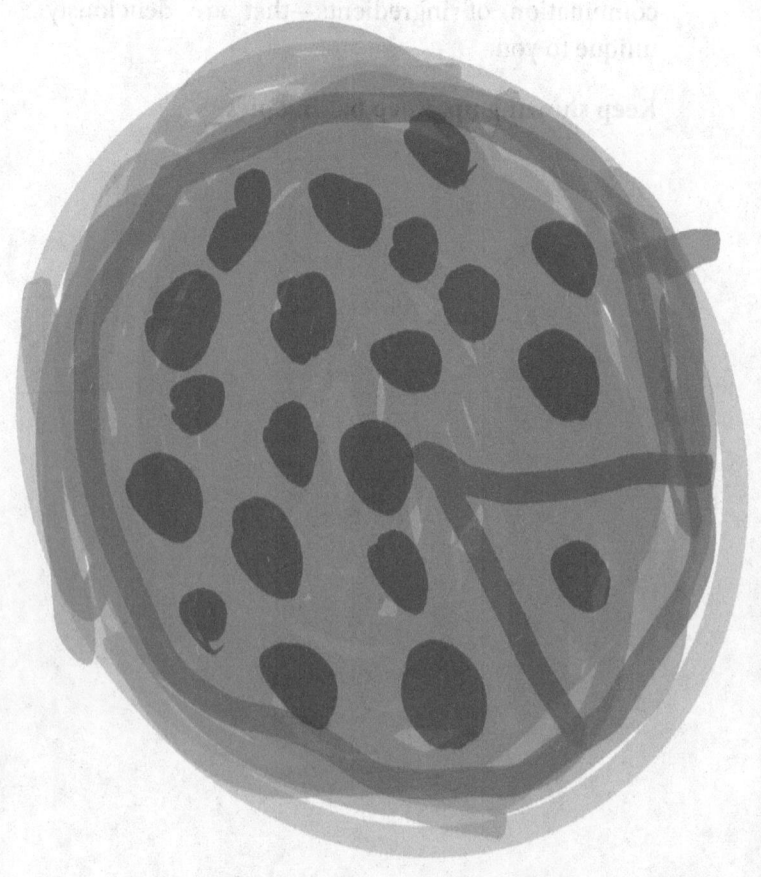

Keep showing up. Keep baking pies.

Keep
showing
up.
Keep
baking
pies.

When children see others drawing, they yearn to jump into the process. The fun is rarely about the output and much more about the inputs: mark making, experimentation, and being part of a creative community.

Show up! Draw pictures! Make pies!

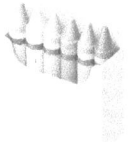

Mother Nature's Curriculum on Creative Practice

Spring has sprung and lessons are in full bloom

"I am not an initiative or a project that can be a success or failure. I am part of nature that gets to be 'alive for a little while."[39] – Brit Chida

Mother Nature selflessly gifts us a bounty of fresh food to keep us healthy, trees to help us breathe, and water to survive. She also provides important lessons that are hidden everywhere in plain sight; Easter eggs for humans to find, adopt, and adapt.

The concept of biomimicry has fascinated me for some time now. Biomimicry is all about looking to existing solutions in nature to solve human problems. For example, Velcro was inspired by the hook-and-loop system naturally found within burr bushes, while the aerodynamic shape of a whale's pectoral fins inspired the design of wind turbine blades.[40] Biomimicry continues to draw me closer to the natural world as I appreciate the small-scale wonders all around me, pondering the lessons nestled within.

Spring Training

I'm no gardener (Certified Cactus Killer here), but as I intentionally slow down in the spring and summer months, I'm more observant about the world around me. Each spring feels like a homecoming, returning to class with Mother Nature as my teacher. Through her beautiful, lush awakening, she reminds me about the timeless lessons related to creative living found within her classroom, often ripe with metaphor. I can't help but sit on the edge of my seat, leaning in and listening intently with all of my senses.

What can Mother Nature's early spring delights teach us about creative practice?

A whole lot, it turns out.

Magnolia Trees

Magnolia trees display beautiful, dramatic blooms early each spring. It always surprises me that such a tropical-looking flower exists on the cusp of winter before anything else has decided to wake from hibernation.

The lessons that Magnolia trees teach us are twofold. First, there are rewards for being the first. When there's little to no competition—even in the form of other greenery, let alone other flowers—Magnolia trees feel like a breath of fresh air; an exciting preview of the abundance ahead. When you take the creative leap early and do what no others are doing, you may be rewarded (internally and externally) for your novelty.

Second, go big or go home. The first blossom of the spring isn't a tiny little sprout or a modest green leaf. It's a huge flowering tree in all shades of pink! Magnolia trees show up unapologetically, and I can't thank them enough for their vulnerability, even in the face of frosty nights.

Hostas

Hosta plants are large and leafy, covering the naked garden soil beautifully. They take little to no effort to care for, which is why they thrive in my garden.

I looked closely at the leaves of a hosta after a heavy rain, and I was amazed to see the efficient system upon which this plant operates. Rainwater sits on the surface of the leaves and is funnelled down the stem to the base of the plant where the water is needed. It's a self-watering plant! Mother Nature shows us that getting systems in place means that I can "set it and forget it."

In his bestselling book *Atomic Habits: An Easy & Proven Way to Build Good Habits & Break Bad Ones,* author James Clear explains the way that making change is less about the individual and more about the system backing the habit. Change the system, change the habit. James reminds us that we don't rise to the level of our goals; rather, we fall to the level of our systems. Flow is enabled with the right system in place.

Green Garden Lilies

As garden lilies begin to rise from the ground, they look a lot like ordinary grass. There's nothing too impressive about them.

The lesson they teach us is that sometimes the simple solution is the best solution. For what garden lilies lack in pizzazz, they more than make up for in practicality. Function over form reigns supreme as they fill the spot in the garden, look great, hide weeds sprouting up beneath them, and need very little attention and care. They look great from the start of spring to the end of fall. Less can be more, plain and simple.

Soloman's Seals

These hearty, leafy stalks are one of my very favourite plants in the garden. They arrive each year taking up the same footprint and growing to the same height as the previous year. For all of their consistency, they have a slow start. But a slow start doesn't mean a slow finish because they grow about a foot in under a week, sprouting up and surpassing the height of all other plants in the garden.

Solomon's seals teach us that there can be a steep learning curve to a new skill or technique, or to the adoption of a new worldview, but once you've begun the journey (starting is often the hardest part!), momentum builds and the results are worth the initial effort.

Less can be more, plain and simple.

Cherry Blossom Trees

Cherry blossoms are visually striking trees that make themselves known through an array of sensory stimuli (namely, colour and smell). Entire festivals are held to celebrate these magnificent trees and the meaning behind them.

As I write this, the final petals are releasing themselves from the cherry blossom tree across the street from my home. I went out of my way to visit this tree today, breathing in a final breath of the season, trying to capture its subtly complex scent. It's one of my very favourite aromas in the entire world, and I must now wait another 350 days until I experience it again.

There are two lessons that cherry blossoms have to share. First, every day is the chance to reinvent yourself. During their brief bloom, cherry blossom trees change with each passing day. Within a few days, they go from vibrant pink to pale pink before all of their petals fall to the ground. The only constant in life is change and the cherry blossom isn't afraid to show up in the world upon sunrise looking decidedly different than it did at the previous sunset. Each new day in the cherry blossom tree's short bloom is a transformation; an awakening.

Second, sometimes there is something so spectacular that happens for such a short time that we must put everything else down to experience it. The blooming period of cherry blossom trees lasts less than two weeks, representing approximately 4 percent of the year. The Japanese phrase *Mono no aware* describes the transience of things;[41] in this case, the feeling when one realizes the beautiful cherry blossoms won't last forever. It's a gentle longing that comes with understanding the blossoms' impermanence; their short existence makes them even *more* beautiful. Creative living ebbs and flows through seasons and there are times when we must remain as present as possible. We'll miss it, unless we stop ruminating on the past, stop planning for the future, and simply stop to smell the roses (or cherry blossoms!). May we carpe that diem and set down our work with the confidence that whatever we put down will be waiting for us when we return.

Tulips

Tulips are a colourful spectacle in early spring. But every year while my neighbour's tulips are in full bloom, mine take a full week or two longer than their counterparts to arrive.

Tulips teach us that things will happen in their own time. Rushing the creative process is inefficient and ineffective, causing frustration along the way. Patience, optimism, and consistency are traits that can create a more fulfilling and abundant creative practice.

Tulips teach us to lean into what feels right. Once our tulips bloomed, I noticed an incredible display taking place. At certain times of the day, the heads of the tulips leaned one way or another. I followed the direction of their lean and was met with the sun. Tulips literally lean into the energy source that fuels them. May we all lean in to the passions, people, processes, and patterns of thinking—online or off—that fuel our energy rather than deplete it.

Dandelions

These pesky little weeds are an annoyance to most, especially those who pride themselves on having a beautiful lawn. However, dandelions have so much hidden wisdom to share, including:

1. *Quantity counts.* With any sort of creative endeavour, it's not just quality that's important—quantity counts too. Making, doing, and figuring it out as you go is only possible if you put in the work. No matter how weedy or annoying dandelions may seem, they've got the quantity thing figured out, and we'd be wise to follow their lead in our own creative practices.

2. *Grit is a choice.* Pick a dandelion and another three will pop up in its place. Their work ethic and unapologetic insistence on showing up is incredible. They show us that we must keep going and that small acts produce huge results. They experience multiple cycles of growth and seed sowing all summer long, continuous action keeping dandelions on display through

three of the four seasons.

3. *Community is critical.* A single dandelion is a weed. A field of dandelions is a beautiful, yellow-spotted living tapestry. From an annoyance to an event, dandelions thrive as part of a larger community. There's magic and connection to be found in the collective.

Three Bonus Plants

As I was looking through photos I've taken over the years, I found three non-spring-specific-yet-highly-relevant plants to share.

Hibiscus

I bought a hibiscus tree on a whim in 2022 because it was so magnificent. She was glorious so I named her Gloria. Gloria bloomed all summer, and if you haven't spent a lot of time around hibiscus trees (like me, before Gloria) you'll be amazed to know that it takes each flower between 30-60 minutes to fully open, blooming only for the day and shriveling up at night, never to be seen again. I was so enraptured by this dramatic process that I took a time lapse video of a bloom opening and I could see the flower moving, willing itself open in a high-energy display.

Beautiful, tropical hibiscus plants have these lessons to teach us:

1. *You're not only as good as your last output.*

A lot of energy is required to produce something beautiful. It's ridiculous for us to expect that each new blossom must be more spectacular than the last, yet that's often how we expect our own creativity to work. More is better. *Better is better.* Instead, it's the incredible spectacle of opening and its limited display that makes the hibiscus so special. There's no need to judge the quality of each individual flower or place unnecessary pressure on the plant to be better and better with each bloom.

2. *Rest is part of the process.* Some days Gloria produced 10 or more blooms and some days she produced none. Much like our own creative practice, the outputs of these trees ebbed and flowed. On days that Gloria didn't produce flowers, I wasn't mad or disappointed because I knew she would bloom again when the time was right.

3. *The creative practice is the art.* Almost as quickly as the blooms arrive, they're gone—but the blooms themselves aren't what's most important. Instead, the entire process that contributed to the final bloom is the work of art. French painter, Yves Klein, viewed his work this way: "My paintings are only the ashes of my art."[42] The final output—the painting, the photograph, the drawing, the song, the dance—is merely the souvenir of our art. Instead, the creative practice and its inputs

(including curiosity, vulnerability, making connections, storytelling) is the art. It's not the final *Mother Nature's Curriculum on Creative Practice* that's most important to me, but rather the idea, conceptualization, imagining, connections, growth, and early morning writing with a soundtrack of orchestral birdsong that are most important. Art need not be defined by *what* is produced, but rather the creative practice of *who, where, when, how and why.*

Mystery Plant

A few years ago, I came across the weirdest and most wonderful plant I'd ever seen. It looked like something strangely Seussian, with its vibrant colour, unusual texture, and fantastical shape. And to this day, I still have no idea what it's called. I went so far as to do a reverse Google image search to name it and even Google was stumped!

I discovered this plant a couple of years ago when I often walked my daughters to a nearby pond in their stroller. The plant was growing out of the side of a hydro box, and it looked so out of place beside the weeds growing on either side of it that I couldn't help but stop and stare. It fascinated me, and I always made a point of admiring it.

The weirdest thing about this plant may not be its appearance or its placement, but rather the fact that it never returned.

Why did it grow? I'll never know. *Oh, the places it could go.* This plant reminded me to "make a ruckus."[43] This is exactly what the mystery plant did—showed up where it wasn't invited and created something of meaning for an audience who cared. For these reasons, it's unforgettable. It also reminded me that weird is wonderful! This plant looked nothing like the plants around it and nothing like I'd ever seen before. It was unique in every way; its weirdness was something to be celebrated, not questioned or criticized. The things that made us weird or unique as kids—perhaps separating us from the herd of our peers—is precisely what our creative practice can highlight and celebrate as adults.

Christmas Cactus

This hearty, blooming succulent is an impressive specimen. We have a Christmas Cactus in our family that is an heirloom. In fact, this healthy, vibrant plant belonged not to my grandmother, nor my great-grandmother but to my great-great-grandmother. Yes, you read that right.

The most important lesson we can learn from this wise, old beauty is that creative longevity is rooted in practice, not performance. The fact that after more than 70 years, it still blooms as magnificently as ever (maybe more so!) should have us pause and invite reflection: how might we make our creative practice

I'm rooting for you!

so worthwhile and so important to us as individuals that we'll want to do it for decades? It's not that we have to create the same outputs, but rather that our practice is so fulfilling that we can see ourselves continuing to engage with creativity far into the future. If it feels more like work than play, it may be time to re-examine what, how, and why we do it. May we engage, explore, and experiment in a way that we can see ourselves *wanting* to do it for a long, long time.

I'm Rooting For You

There is so much to learn about creative practice from Mother Nature's blossoming curriculum. Plants in early spring and beyond remind us that:

- There are rewards for putting yourself out there before anyone else and being unapologetically vulnerable.
- Establishing systems to make habit formation easier can benefit our creative practice.
- Less is often more.
- Momentum builds over time and the results are worth the hard work of overcoming a steep learning curve.
- Every day is a chance to reinvent oneself.
- It's sometimes necessary to jump into something fully, making the most of a short-term opportunity.
- Things will happen in their own time.

- It's important to lean into the energies that fuel us.
- Quantity begets quality in creative work: do, learn, grow, improve, do, learn, grow, improve…
- Grit is a choice.
- Community is critical.
- You aren't only as good as your last output.
- Rest is part of the process.
- Inputs of our creative practice are just as important—maybe more important—as the outputs.
- Make meaning for an audience who cares.
- Weird is wonderful!
- Creative practice should feel more like play than work.
- Focus on the process over the performance for a long, creatively fulfilling existence.

The next time you're out for a walk, pause to consider what nature can teach us about creativity. What human-made problems have already been solved through Mother Nature's majesty?

Some crayons are bold and bright, while other crayons are deep and dark. Some are freshly sharpened, while others are worn from heavy use. Yet they exist side-by-side in the same box, each occupying its own place in the group. Their true magic lies not in sameness, but in their differences—an interdependency of colours: blending, contrasting, and complementing one another to create what no single crayon could achieve alone.

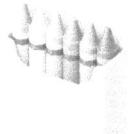

Certainty and Mysticism

Surrendering intellect to know the unknowable

I recently saw author Elizabeth Gilbert speak to 2000+ Toronto-based fans and she was incredible. We listened to her tell new stories, as well as familiar ones told from new angles. What's stuck with me is one particular topic she channelled: mysticism.

Liz spoke about Richard from Texas (chronicled in her memoir, *Eat Pray Love*) and the way in which his calm, relaxed *it's gonna be alright* attitude was a direct result of everything not being alright. In a suicide attempt that should have been the end, Richard had a spiritual awakening between the states of life and death, hearing a voice tell him that everything was going to be alright. When he awoke from that experience, he not only believed this statement to be true, but also embodied it in his demeanour, mindset, and actions.

Liz also spoke about her beloved Rayya, whom she lost to pancreatic and liver cancers in 2018. She recalled some of the most challenging, painful, helpless moments during Rayya's final weeks. Through all of the excruciating pain of seeing her love suffer, she fondly recalled Rayya's final breath, which brought the happiest, most wondrous expression to her face. Liz has no way of knowing what Rayya saw, but she knows it was beautiful.

The in-between—from here to there, earthside to another side—is a mystery to all of us. Sometimes the world is curious and beautiful and unknowable, and that's exactly the way things should be.

Creative Confidence

In thinking about creative confidence, creativity itself may be seen as a mystical experience. In her book *Big Magic: Creative Living Beyond Fear*, Liz Gilbert talks about the way she's devoted her life to creativity and offers a unique, magical understanding of its origin:

> *"I am referring to the supernatural, the mystical, the inexplicable, the surreal, the divine, the transcendent, the other-worldly. Because the truth is I believe that creativity is a force of enchantment, not entirely human in its origins."*[44]

In a creative heart-to-heart with his wife Suleika Jaouad, celebrated musician and artist Jon Batiste said this about creativity:

> *"Creativity is mysterious. Creativity has something to do with craft but it also has more to do with life. Creativity is something that is a steady stream in the subconscious realm; in the realm of the spirit."*[45]

Alternatively, confidence suggests the requirement of a more human-centred, down-to-earth mindset about what we do and make. Certainty is "the state of being completely confident or having no doubt about something,"[46] appears to be in direct opposition to unknowable, unseeable mysticism.

Confidence suggests the requirement of a more human-centred, down-to-earth mindset about what we do and make.

But here's the magic at play: it doesn't have to be just one or the other—mysticism or certainty—in the pursuit of a more creatively confident existence. There's room to play in the grey between both sides of the spectrum. We don't have to have it all figured out in order to experience joy and love and pain and humanity and inspiration and intuition.

When we acknowledge that multiple truths exist, a third path makes itself available; we can choose to be certain about surrendering intellect to know the unknowable, embracing all that the universe has to offer.

Just Like Grandad

My dad, Rob, was a guy with a big heart who loved a good head scratch.

He spent nearly 20 years volunteering his free time and musical talents to a local church. He never missed an opportunity to talk about my accomplishments. As a teenager, it was mortifying, but I now realize he was just so proud of me. That pride grew to include my daughter, Charlotte, who was eleven months old when my dad received his diagnosis: advanced pancreatic cancer. He was given less than four months to live.

Although a very difficult battle, my father lived 16 months past his diagnosis, and in that time he learned that he'd soon be expecting a second grandchild. In a conversation with my husband, my dad entrusted him with his greatest regret—that he would likely not have the strength to meet her.

In his final days, I was prepared for his bedridden state, but I wasn't prepared to lose my dad as I'd always known him. He built his career in sales and was a performer his entire life. ("Mic check, mic check" were practically my first words.) When he stopped being able to speak, it was a monumental shift and only Charlotte could get a response from her grandad—the turn of his head, a difficult-to-muster smile, a tiny wave. During his final days, I turned on 1970s rock 'n' roll music, and I know if he was able to, he could tell me the name of each song, each artist, each release date. We listened to his favourite songs and I stroked his hair, trying to put on a brave face, knowing he would soon be outside of the body that was failing him so badly.

On March 1, 2019, I lost my father.

It was 27 days before my second daughter was born, and during that time, there was a palpable sense of the in-between. My dad was no longer in this world, but my daughter wasn't yet either. I wanted to believe that on some unknown and yet-to-be-understood level, the two spent the entire time together—my dad playing his guitar with his second granddaughter gleefully tapping the matching ukulele, just as had happened earthside with his first. And it's the strangest thing—in my memory of my dad's final days, I have no recollection of my nearly nine-months-pregnant belly.

On March 28, a new little life arrived, and we named her Hannah *Robin*.

Just like Grandad.

In the weeks that followed, we learned that she loved music. It seemed to feed her soul more than it ever had our first daughter.

Just like Grandad.

In the months that followed, Hannah began playing with her hair to soothe herself to sleep, completely unprompted and unprovoked like it was the most natural thing in the world. It's something she still does to this day. She uses her little fingers to help drift from a state of joyful consciousness into peaceful, deep sleep.

Just like Grandad.

Lending Voice to the In-Between

My dad's favourite creative medium was audio.

As a seven-year-old, I have memories of him pulling out blueprints, explaining a schematic of a sound system installation to my grade two peers (which, for obvious reasons, went over everyone's head).

As a 15-year-old, I have memories of every floor of our house reverberating with rock 'n' roll as my dad's band practised for an upcoming gig.

As a 29-year-old, I have memories of his rigorous sound checks before my wedding to ensure the audio was *jussssssst* right.

Music and sound were a huge part of his life and, therefore, a huge part of mine.

Like a family heirloom, I've long held onto an audio recording of my dad and I reading my favourite childhood book together, recorded in the late 1980s. I've always known—deep down in my creative intuition—that there would be more to its story.

I don't think it's a coincidence that I began working with audio as a creative medium (podcasting) in the same year I lost my dad. And while he never got the chance to meet his youngest granddaughter, we now have the chance to hear them read together for the first and last time.

Here's *Put Me In the Zoo (Part 2!),* uniting grandfather and granddaughter through the certainty of audio and the mysticism of creativity.

Crayons contain certain and mystical potential. They can transform a blank page into virtually anything, leaping from nothingness to somethingness. The blending and layering of colours and shades not visible in the original colour palette is a delightful side effect of creative exploration in this medium.

As an experiment in certainty and mysticism, try covering the page with colours of all kinds, ensuring that a thick layer of crayon wax covers the page. Next, paint the whole page black, wait for it to dry, and then use a sharp object (like a paper clip) to scratch an image onto the page to reveal the rainbow of colours underneath. It's certain that the colours exist underneath, but precisely which ones will be exposed and how they will work together is completely, magically uncertain.

Into the Deep

Glub, glub

Like so many around the world, I use the start of the new calendar year to think about where I'm headed and what I'd like to bring into the days ahead. I'm less focused on resolutions and more focused on a word or phrase, as well as visual imagery that will help me understand my values and what's most important. For nearly a decade, I've made annual 11" x 17" posters that contain small rectangles with imagery, each symbolizing promises and reminders to myself.

To my surprise, the weeks leading up to 2024 were a little different. It was mid-December, and I was in the middle of finishing up my grading and admin work for the semester, getting ready for Christmas and feeling nearly burnt out when I was overcome with the desire to create my new year poster.

The concept came to me quickly, and it didn't look like any of my other posters. It felt more visceral and authentic and interesting than in past years. I whipped it up in only a few minutes, and I didn't change a thing once the text made it to the page.

Then, a few weeks later in mid-January 2024, the strangest thing happened. I was overcome with a desire and intuition to write poetry. Poetry. (Poetry?!?) I've never written poetry in my life. It was 9:30 p.m. and I was in my dark kitchen toasting myself half a bagel with peanut butter and jam when the poetry wave washed over me.

2024

into the deep

presence | embodiment | slowness
time | expansion | molasses | less

I think a lot about the brilliant Liz Gilbert and her beliefs on the magic of creative ideas and intuition. She's described the way so many wonderful creative people throughout history talk about moments of creative inspiration, often in delightfully unexpected or surprising ways.

So, if my creative genius decides to visit me on a peanut butter-filled Thursday evening, who am I to question it?

The three poems that poured out of me all relate to my 2024 intention: into the deep. I am immensely proud of this kitchen-table poetry, and I share this not to brag about my new-found skills (who knows if I'll ever be able to replicate the poetic creative flow I experienced?!), but to share with you my feelings of joy; unexpected creative forces working behind the scenes in mysterious and wonderful ways, reaffirming their presence and their willingness to play.

Into the Deep

Into the deep

I sink deeper

      deeper

          deeper

              down.

    Stillness.

    Silence.

There is nothing here.

There is everything here,

waiting to be found.

Relativity

My high school
music teacher once said:
"Everything is relative."

These 3 words visit me
more often than they should for 3 words
uttered half a lifetime ago.

But these 3 words hold
universal truth felt by me,
felt by worlds.

Everything
is
relative.

When I sit in the depths—
not forcing the withholding of breath
but inviting it to take a breath of its own—

Is when time s l   o   w   s.
Is when noise quiets.
Is when I feel *still*.

It is here that I witness
everything is—indeed—relative.
And I am grateful.

Thirst

A deep, complex thirst wells up inside of me constantly
for   This
          That
          The other

I've tried to quench this needy thirst
with   This
          That
          The other

And it always almost always works.

But this eternal internal thirst
is never satisfied. Never goes away.
Never.

Which makes total sense
because, of course,
this forever thirst
cannot be fooled into
the molding of a modern world.

This un-thirstable thirst
can never be fulfilled
through consuming
outside of myself.

This ancient thirst is older
than me,
than you,
than the dinosaurs,
than the universe.

This wise thirst requires
the immersion,
the swallowing
of myself
into something bigger
outside of myself, still.

This unshakable thirst
understands
even if I don't.

And as I begin to

       sink

              into myself

       into the something bigger

I suddenly
don't feel
very thirsty.

I am free.

A blue crayon may glide across the page to represent water, but true depth isn't found in hurried strokes. True depth is found in the places where the crayon lingers, pressing deeper, layer upon layer, until the colour becomes richer, darker, and more profound. Creativity, like the sea, reveals its magic in the sinking below the surface, where knowing replaces searching, and where the deepest blues are possible.

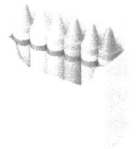

HUN

"What if we measured true success not by the amount of money you have but by the amount of human energy you unlock, the amount of potential you enable? If that were our metric, our world would be a different place."[47] – Jacqueline Novogratz

> May we work together to find the keys that will turn the world on its axis.

Less Strategy, More Humanity

Create from the inside out, resisting the urge to create from the outside in

Let's talk about strategy.

There's strategy to foster click-throughs, strategy to elicit likes, strategy to build engagement, strategy to boost sharing, and strategy to drive performance.

Strategy is exhausting.

Humans weren't built to act like machines, focused on ever-advancing statistics to validate our collective being; yet, many of us spend our days focused on developing strategies to build our self-worth this way.

I understand the appeal.

Digital metrics of success are so much easier to understand and quantify in the face of more meaningfully messy measures. They satisfy our "fast thinking" with immediate gratification and straightforward answers. 20 likes? Great! 200 likes? Even better! There's a linear correlation that makes our dopamine skyrocket alongside the digital approval.

Marketing Loses Its Appeal

I've spent the last 20 years of my life learning about, creating, and working alongside the space of digital marketing. But the more strategies and metrics I learn, the more I'm trying to separate myself from them.

I say this not to speak ill of the marketers doing their jobs, but to acknowledge a tilt of my internal axis, from the need for external validation that feeds my ego to an internal knowing that more directly feeds my soul.

It's not to say that I won't post anything self-promotional ever again, but it's the constant drive to create for an audience that feels performative. Nor is it to say that I'm immune to quick and easy metrics. I still feel the pull towards the (illusion of) validation they bring. But I'm feeling the icks.

And when I eased off trying to prove my worth to others, a shift—a quieting—happened inside of me.

This quiet contemplation, the rising desire for humility, a sense of enoughness, fostering community—this all feels way more important to me than marketing ever has or ever will.

A few years ago, I had the pleasure of speaking with Meg Lewis, an artist, performer, and educator who transforms the world through joy and playful design. I love their take on understanding your personal style, both inside and out. They shared that this can help drive so many life decisions, and it proves to be so much more fulfilling than trying to follow trends, both in fashion and in life. Meg shared that it's taken a long time for them to come to this place of inner knowing about their style, their work, and their why.

And when I eased off trying to prove my worth to others, a shift—a quieting—happened inside of me.

The more I deepen my learning and practice of creative confidence, the more I believe unequivocally that it comes not from external statistics, but from a deep, internal knowing.

Knowing who we are.

Knowing what we like.

Knowing that we are worth it, in all the ways we show up in this world.

Knowing that we mean a lot to a small group of people, rather than meaning a little to a lot of people.

Knowing oneself so deeply that even though outside metrics exist, they don't interrupt important thoughts shared by your inner voice.

Turning Metrics Inside Out

How do we take the external metrics many of us have become accustomed to and turn them inward, making them work for our creativity instead of against it?

1. **Click through** past projects you've created and select 3-5 that you can review.
2. Choose one to start and point out all the things you **like** about your own work. Take one piece and list all of the reasons you chose it. Every single thing, no matter how small or insignificant it may seem. Move onto the next piece, and do it again and again until you've

exhausted all possible ideas. Be generous and kind to yourself.

3. **Engage** with yourself and with your creative process, committing to blocking out time daily, weekly, or monthly to give your creativity breathing room. Turn off all devices and remove distractions during these blocks of focused creative time.
4. **Share** your past self with your present self by looking back at old journals you've written in. One of my favourite collaborators is my past self on the pages of my notebooks.
5. **Check in** with your friends and creative confidants to learn what they're up to and how you can support one another.

A final note: It's wonderful when what we are *paid to do* intersects with what we feel we are *meant to do*. Even if this doesn't describe your situation, there's lots of magic to be found in a creative side hustle—not for money, but for expression, experimentation, and expansiveness that can come from creative making. Start small, build slowly, wander aimlessly, and find joy in the journey. Do so with the mindset to create from the inside out, resisting the urge to create from the outside in, so that we may feel the deep satisfaction that only we can give ourselves.

A crayon doesn't wait for the paper to tell it what to be. It simply colours. It doesn't need permission to be bold, soft, warm, or bright. When we create from the inside out, we're not trying to meet external expectations. Instead, we're letting what's already inside of us shine through.

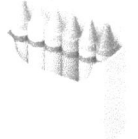

The Opposite of Perfection

is not imperfection

Perfection is subjective.

Perfection is relative.

Perfection is not real.

One of my favourite things about creative work is that outputs exist in all forms on a *continuum*. There's multiple correct solutions and multiple truths that emerge in response to a single creative problem. Right and wrong, black and white, yes and no don't need to exist in spaces that require creative problem-solving; there's lots of room in the middle to play.

The Cambridge Dictionary defines perfection as: "the state of being complete and correct in every way."[48]

Perfection can be such a dangerous trap in creative work because we see examples of incredible (seemingly perfect) work all around us. This work has found its audience, and I'm happy for this work, but I'm also aware that many are critical of it. What appears flawless to one will be flawed to another; it's all about perspective. A unanimous, quantitative, collective idea of "perfect" just isn't possible.

I appreciate the ideas of celebrated artist and writer, Lisa Congdon about why perfection is problematic. In May 2024 at the DesignThinkers Vancouver conference, she affirmed her belief that perfection isn't real because it's based on our perception of how we *think* others will like our work, which is a dangerous and unnecessary assumption: *"Perfection is a bi-product of binary thinking. Perfectionism, at its core, is a fear of not being good enough or good in a way you think your work should be good, which is based on years of learning from dominant culture about what constitutes good, which shuts us off from learning and makes it harder to change or for our work to evolve."*[49]

Perfectionist tendencies are often rooted in an honourable place—a desire to do our best work and be our most "fully-realized selves." However, perfectionism's downfall lies in its focus on the end result and how others will respond to it. Fear of failure, fear of being judged, fear of uncertainty, fear of not aligning with our identities...all of it sets us up to fall short of (our own) expectations. After all, we can only control our process, not what happens after we release something into the world.

So if perfection isn't real and not a helpful goal, what's the alternative?

The Opposite of Perfection is Not Imperfection

It's contentment.

When we see perfection in creative work for what it is (a primarily externally-imposed, unrealistic, unhelpful goal), we can embrace the countercultural, internally-motivated, softer, wiser path of *contentment*. Instead of chasing perfection and the pursuit of our "next best self," what if we relish in our current contentment? Contentment for where

A unanimous, quantitative, collective idea of "perfect" just isn't possible.

we are right now and what we have in this moment.

If perfection feels like a stifling little box we must squeeze ourselves into, contentment feels like a spacious breath of fresh mountain air.

In a perspective-shifting conversation about neurodiversity for the *Ologies with Alie Ward* podcast, author Jessica McCabe (of *How to ADHD*) shared this about perfectionism: *"It can be paralyzing for people who are neurodivergent to even want to go out and try things and interact because we've been corrected so often our whole lives that we're so afraid to mess up. We almost get trained into being perfectionists because we keep getting corrected and we keep being told 'that's wrong' [...] that's a terrible way to live. Like just constantly being afraid of messing up because then you don't want to take the shot, right?"*[50]

Prioritizing finding joy in the journey and making progress along the way is important for both neurodivergent and neurotypical brains. It's a much more light-hearted, pressure-free, confidence-boosting mindset than striving for perfection will ever be.

And the irony is that once we begin to approach our work with more joy, lightness, and authenticity—*contentment*—chances are we won't only enjoy the process more but our outcomes will also be of higher quality as our sense of possibilities expands with our mindset.

First is the Worst

My creative backlog is bustling; I've got a long list of places to go, people to see, and ideas to explore. If I try to make any one thing "perfect," I'm robbing myself of time and energy that could be used to pursue other ideas.

I'm not suggesting that we put less energy into a project than it deserves or rush for the sake of producing lots of work, but rather that we recognize that *good and done* is better than *perfect and not done*. I try to finish projects with contentment, knowing that they could always be better (because creative work is inherently iterative), and I'm proud of my creation, or at least proud of having seen it through.

For example, in episode 001 of my podcast *Talk Paper Scissors*, I told listeners that I hoped my first episode would be my worst episode. I knew I would learn from each and every one I made thereafter, deepening my understanding of the relationship between quality and practice. The only way I was going to get better was to put in the work.

Can I look back on that first episode and find 87 things wrong with it?

Yes.

Can I also look back on that first episode with excitement and pride that I did it, that I released it out into the world, allowing me to produce 227 episodes (and counting!) after it, learning from each one?

YES.

But no matter the pride we feel for what we've made and how far we've come, how do we forgive ourselves for what we didn't know at the time? How do we overcome feelings of guilt or shame about our flawed past work?

Singer and songwriter Jake Wesley Rogers believes that creative living requires both self-esteem *and* self compassion. In moments where his self-esteem is lacking, his self-compassion steps in to hold him up.

I wholeheartedly agree that moments of self-esteem can come and go, but creative stick-with-it-ness requires us to be gentle and accepting of ourselves, no matter the outcome.

May we intentionally honour our past, take pride in our present, and remain open to our future.

May we practise and try things and make stuff, letting our work live in the world *perfectly imperfectly*.

May we remember that perfection is limiting, while contentment is expansive.

Good and done is better than perfect and not done.

Good
and done
is better
than
perfect
and not
done.

"I'm not that sharp," said the crayon.

"I'm not that bright," said the pencil.

Yet, the world is a better place for each having displayed their unique, imperfect gifts.

Practice Makes Progress

Less power-walking, more dancing

"Practice makes perfect" is such a common phrase that Google auto-completed it after I typed "practice" and the letter "m."

But practice doesn't make perfect because perfect is an unhelpful illusion in creative work. Instead, practice makes *progress.*

Practice is important because it's through the act of *doing* that we figure out what works and what doesn't. Practice allows us to try and succeed—or try and fail—inherently breeding confidence with each stroke of the paintbrush, type of the keyboard, mix of cookie dough, or rehearsal of a dance routine. Once we become more aware of a subject matter, tool, or technique, we become more comfortable sharing it with the world in the form of our creative outputs.

Practice doesn't always feel like progress in the moment, but it becomes visible over time. Creativity is non-linear and it's messy, but when we zoom out we gain enough perspective to appreciate the journey—one with a looping, upwards trajectory.

On Reading and Writing

I have always been an *okay* writer. I'm someone who had to write, rewrite, and then rewrite again before it was ready. It never felt possible for me to write a clean first draft with my ideas in a logical order.

Even when I began writing professionally in 2008, I still considered myself an average writer who took *forever* to finalize a good copy.

It wasn't until I was forced to write under serious time constraints that I became a stronger writer. It was in 2013, and I had just started my graduate degree, during which I was taking two three-week intensive courses at the same time. I would attend class all day, and then return to the space I was renting on the University of Alberta's campus to read and write long responses to complex prompts. This was on top of the assignments, papers, and projects required to successfully complete the courses. I had no time to question my writing ability or mull over imperfection.

I credit this intense practice with getting me over the hump and forcing me to get out of my own way.

I became a stronger writer, five years *after* I began writing professionally. I've become an even faster, stronger, more confident writer since, strictly due to the quantity I write. I'm definitely not perfect (I'm currently on the fourth round of edits on my book), but consistent practice has made progress, bit-by-bit.

On Reading My Writing

Much like my first podcast episode, I could look back on my first articles and point out all the flaws, knowing that it's inferior work by my standards today and cringing at the thought that it's readily available on the internet. But this is what relinquishing control over the final outcome is all about, and this

But practice doesn't make perfect because perfect is an unhelpful illusion in creative work. Instead, practice makes *progress*.

is when our bravery and self-compassion is needed most—when we're separated from our past work by months, years, or even decades.

I've felt steady progress, and knowing that my work will never be perfect, I choose *contentment*—simultaneously honouring my past writing, taking pride in my present writing, and remaining open to my future writing.

Quality *and* quantity count in creative work because with quantity comes quality; the latter could not exist without the former. Both are needed and both matter.

Cha Cha Cha

If you're anything like me, when it comes to making time to practise, some days you're completely in the zone. Things are working smoothly, you've got ideas coming from every direction, and things are happening. *Two steps forward...*

But as with all ebbs and flows in life, there are days when I just. feel. stuck. Nothing is quite going right, and I don't feel motivated to make anything creative. *One step back...*

My creativity comes in spurts. Sometimes all I can do is wait for my next idea, priming my brain by reading, listening, walking, and taking in all of the sensory information that will inspire me. And when the inspiration comes, it often arrives in a crazy downpour. I turn my umbrella upside down, trying to catch as many ideas as I possibly can.

During these intense periods of creative flow, I can write 2000 or 3000 coherent, meaningful words at a time. Other days, words I struggle exit brain through fingers and page doesn't fill good, oof.

I know my creativity works this way, and I don't panic when it doesn't clock in during business hours. I rest assured knowing that my next idea and flow state will come in its own time. I have to be patient and give myself lots of time to let things marinate, working to my own internal deadlines long before external ones come due.

None of us can be our most creative selves all the time, and I think this is an important part of the process; without the lows, we wouldn't know the highs. For example, when I originally wrote these words, I had a screaming toddler at my knees who was mad for a reason I couldn't figure out, a preschooler refusing to play at the park, and an active dog pulling at my hip leash wanting to sniff everything in sight. I had not accomplished close to what I wanted that day, but getting frustrated wasn't going to solve any problems.

I decided that the day was less of a power walk forward and more of a lighthearted dance around my creative practice.

Two steps forward, one step back, one to the side! Let's dance! Cha! Cha! Cha!

Crayons are the ideal tool for embracing progress over perfection. They aren't made for precision, which naturally leaves space for play, experimentation, and joy in the process. Their charm lies in the freedom they offer.

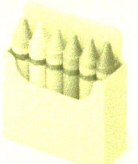

Laugh Lines

Changing the narrative, one story at a time

I was helping my seven-year-old brush her teeth and get ready for bed. We caught a glance of each other in the mirror when she stopped.

"What are those marks beside your mouth?" she asked, pointing to the lines beginning to make themselves visible on my 38-year-old face.

I knew I had an important choice to make:

1. Explain that they're called wrinkles, and they appear as you get older. And that many women try to avoid them at all costs because they're a sign of aging, which we are told is a socially-unacceptable state of being in most cultures where young, beautiful skin is preferred at all costs.
2. Tell a different story.

"These are called laugh lines. I've worked really hard to get them. I've laughed A LOT to make them appear."

She looked at me for a second, trying to process this new information. Seemingly satisfied with my answer, she turned and walked out of the bathroom towards her bed where I caught a faint sound of deliberate joy. She was giggling to herself as she crawled into bed, putting in her time so that one day her lines might appear, too.

Wrinkled paper is evidence of exuberant existence; it's proof of life in the joyful act of creating.

Reflective Recalibration

Running a 26.2-mile marathon requires a different pace than sprinting a 100-yard dash

There's a lot of media attention about the concept of "quiet quitting."

Quiet quitting is about doing only what's required at work—putting in the required daily hours and using minimal effort. Taking on out-of-scope work or volunteering for committees, for example, is not for quiet quitters.

I can appreciate both arguments:

1. Do what you're paid to do, do it to spec, go home, have a life.
2. Go above and beyond, try new things, meet new people, develop your skill set across teams, go home, have a little less of a life in the name of long-term growth.

I'll admit that I've spent the majority of my life firmly planted in the second camp, which has benefited me greatly but has also had its drawbacks. This is particularly true as I enter my 15th year of work, raising a young family, after having experienced a multi-year pandemic.

The time for introspection is upon me.

RR > QQ

I'm very fortunate to love what I do, having a deep passion for teaching, visual communication, and the intersection of the two. I know not everyone works in a job they enjoy, and I'm hugely privileged in this position. Even still, it's time for me to re-examine how I spend my days, which, after all, is how I spend my weeks, my months, my years and ultimately, my life.

I definitely don't want to quietly quit, but I *must* **reflectively recalibrate.**

This means looking closely at all facets of my job, doubling down on the things that add the most value to students, and scaling back things I'm doing because I've "always done it that way". It also requires reviewing my scope of work and specifically what's expected of me.

I consider myself a recovering people pleaser and competitive overachiever. I often take on too much, but do so from hopeful excitement.

Reflective recalibration means that I *might* take on out-of-scope work, *but* I'm much more selective about what I take on, knowing that my time and energy are finite resources. I'll pause before taking on a non-essential project (revolutionary for me!), and I'll move forward only if it's inherently enjoyable or interesting, letting curiosity be my guide. If it's not a "Heck yes!" it's a "No, thank you!". Feeling obligated out of a sense of guilt is no longer part of my worry wheelhouse. I know that I need to pace myself for the sake of the quality of my work and quality time with family.

Reflective recalibration means that I *might* take on out-of-scope work, *but* I'm much more selective about what I take on, knowing that my time and energy are finite resources.

Scaling back my out-of-scope work has also allowed me to explore creative passion projects outside of my day job. Sometimes these are just for me, and sometimes they have spilled over into paid work opportunities. Either way, exploring these passion projects means I come to my day job in a better place to fulfill my in-scope duties—a little more pep in my step and a little more clear-headed, knowing I'm being more thoughtful in my decisions. This makes me feel lighter, which makes me better at my job. (Full circle moment!)

So, the moral of my story is that there is a happy medium between full-on quiet quitting and continuing to sprint like it's a 100-yard dash in a marathon that's 26.2 miles long. A reflective recalibration requires zooming out to see the bigger picture and recognizing that people pleasing by placing productivity on a pedestal will hurt us as individuals—and organizations as large collections of individuals—unless we reflectively recalibrate.

That's why you'll find me staying in my own lane, pacing myself in my own race, content with the reflective recalibration that got me here. After all, as Bob Marley reminds us, "The day you stop racing, is the day you win the race."[51]

Restlessness

Sometimes, upon reflection, days feel difficult and stunted and frustrating. Today I feel unsettled, restless, and lacking sturdiness.

I have everything I need in this world and more: shelter, safety, food, family, fulfilling paid work, and volunteerism. (I'm practically dancing on the summit of Maslow's pyramid, baby!)

Yet, my eye twitch has returned.

An unmet need, no matter how deeply ingrained, is undoubtedly restless. There is something askew, something missing.

Also, I'm certain I'm not the only one with an itch because scratchy solutions are promised everywhere: promises from highly-targeted and cleverly crafted ads on mass and social media; a buffet of ever-evolving tools, tricks, and courses available on demand.

But I know, deep down, that *the something* can't be solved by any outside means or by anyone other than myself. In my 37 years on planet Earth, I'm only beginning to understand that solutions to complex problems come not from having more answers, but from *asking more questions.* Solutions are often found by talking less and *listening more.* Solutions make themselves known not through trying to control a situation, but by believing with unwavering conviction that *connection is the ultimate goal.*

Solutions arise not from knowing more, but *knowing that there's so much more to know.*

Without fail, when you're looking for something you begin to see it everywhere—also known as the Baader-Meinhof Phenomenon or the Frequency Illusion.[52] You think about the red car your family had growing up and, all of a sudden, red cars are everywhere on the roads. It's as though a filter has been placed on top of the contents of life, capturing *the something*.

What's ever-present for me right now are ideas about calmness, encouragement of stillness, and the value of more from less. For example, these three works have caught my attention, having been caught in my filter this week:

- An article from *Becoming Minimalist* entitled "The One Hour Each Week That Will Change Your Life for the Better—Every Time."
- A copy of Patrick Rhone's 2012 book *enough,* which I found while cleaning up other paperwork.
- My weekly instalment of the brilliant Substack *Letters From Love with Elizabeth Gilbert*—this week's letter answering the question, "Dear Love, what would you have me know today about finding a sense of calm?"

Tellingly, Liz's Letters From Love practice has been on my to-do list for years. In this daily ritual, she asks love/spirit/the universe "what would you have me know today?" letting the words pour out of her—not consciously *from* her, but *through* her. My procrastination with starting this practice has run rampant (out of fear, perhaps?), but when Liz recently started her Substack community, I felt encouraged to finally give it a go. While I've only written three short letters so far, each one feels like an outstretched hand towards internal stillness. It feels like an actionable solution that can only be found through asking questions, listening to the answers, and striving for connection, knowing that *I know very little.*

I share them with you here in hopes that we may connect—across time and space—over a shared restlessness. And in the sturdiness of connection, may we find a sliver of stillness.

Dear Love, what would you have me know today?

01/11/24

There is nothing that I can tell you that you do not already know. I am inside of you. I am you. There are moments you may feel tired, exasperated, but I am still here.

Gratitude is like a key that unlocks me and my unwavering presence is known, again and again. But gratitude feels elusive, like flossing. I know it's important to my overall health and well-being, yet, like flossing, it's forgotten or passed over for sleeping, eating, sitting, working or literally any other excuse.

Here's what I want you to know about gratitude: sit close, listening even more closely and breathe in.

That's it. Breathe in. That's gratitude.

Remove the excuse of overcomplicating the process, instead surrendering to the doing, the breathing. Unlike flossing, there are no special tools required, or a bathroom mirror in which to see your progress. Instead, I will be your mirror. But you don't even need me to explicitly show you your progress because this mirror is inside of you.

This mirror is you.

So then all you must do is sit, sit close, listening, observing, remaining present, and breathe. In and out, strong and unencumbered with ease and with life-giving force.

For this, I am grateful.

01/14/24

Stillness is vital to living.

May we ebb and flow, ebb and flow.

The ebbing is just as much a part of the process as flowing.

Sit, still, settled.

Love is found in stillness.

The simplest, yet most difficult thing is moving ahead by not moving.

Be still.

03/16/24

There is a deep restlessness inside. Moving, churning, itching for more. You want to close your eyes, bringing stillness to the end of the day.

Guilt will pass. Forgiveness will come.

In the stillness. In the stillness.

Don't consume; be consumed.

Be still, just rest, for tomorrow is another glorious, hope-filled day.

Goodnight.

A crayon worn down to a dull stub doesn't stop being useful; perhaps it just needs a moment to collect itself and be re-sharpened. Creativity works the same way. When ideas feel stuck or uninspired, it's not a sign to stop; it's a cue to pause, reflect, and recalibrate. A fresh edge, a new angle…and suddenly, the crayon is ready to glide again, as bold and confident as ever.

Restlessness

~~Dear Love,~~
~~what will you have me know today?~~

Two important things have been caught in my awareness filter in the 48 hours since I hit publish on the original piece about restlessness, and this redacted reimagining will make more sense once I explain what I've discovered.

Important Thing #1

Yesterday, on my commute home from work, I stumbled upon the most recent episode of the podcast *Unlocking Us* with Brené Brown, entitled "Esther Perel on the new AI—Artificial Intimacy." There were so many beautiful ideas shared between the two powerhouse thinkers, and I feverishly scribbled down notes while listening on the train.

One idea stood out amongst the rest (caught in my filter!), which is the notion that we're currently living "beyond human scale." Many of us are tethered to technology by work and by choice—connected to a vast array of people and places, performing on social media to thousands of followers, and tapped into a network beyond our human cognitive capacity. Their conversation weaved in and out of beautiful stories and thoughtful lines of questioning, exploring what it means to stay human in a hyper-connected world that's decidedly un-human in structure.

Aha! That's it!

There's a restlessness that comes from operating *beyond human scale.*

No amount of colourful schedules, optimized workflows, or creative outputs can quiet the restlessness. These systems facilitate connection within large networks, perpetuating my struggle to operate beyond what my human brain has evolved to effectively cope with. I don't think it's all bad (not in the least), but there's a tipping point…perhaps it's when computer and phone interaction surpass human interaction in a 24-hour period? There's something deep and meaningful and profound here. This feels like it's at the root of my restlessness.

Important Thing #2

I love going to art therapy because it often feels like a creative improv session. I'll be prompted to answer a question in a unique way (often using found materials and objects in my space) and when and how I respond often sparks discussion that leads to other questions and additional creative prompting.

It's a dialogue, and it's also a dance.

My art therapist and I were discussing the contents of my writing about restlessness. We discussed the stillness, and the rest and ebbing that I'm craving. As a prompt, they asked me to choose a book from my bookshelf with a cover that felt like the kind of rest I was looking for. I found one with two simple, brightly coloured concentric circles with big, sturdy, simple text (yes, we use typography analogies in art therapy).

On my shelf, I also found the incredible book *Tree of Codes* by Jonathan Safran Foer, which felt like a metaphor for the process of getting to stillness. To create his book, Jonathan brilliantly took the original book *The Street of Crocodiles* by Bruno Shulz and physically cut away at the text to create a new story within the original. The result is a book that was incredibly difficult to manufacture because each one of its 130+ pages is uniquely die-cut.

My clever art therapist (dancing the dance) invited me to make a copy of "Restlessness" and use the same redactive process that Jonathan used to chip away at my own words, leaving only the most relevant behind.

The result is fewer words and a new story within the original.

Through this process of leaning on my beloved books as visual symbols, I discovered that less can be a great path to a solution. It's not always a top-of-mind solution when our schooling, interactions, and professional lives encourage more. Less can feel simple—too simple—but there's a resonant energy present in less.

If the process of solving through less were represented in sound, it would be quiet, slow, and calm—juxtaposed against the sound of solving through more, which I interpret as loud, excited, and frenetic. There's a place for both, but I'm grateful to be reminded that less is an option.

I am calmed by the prospect of less.

I am stilled by the prospect of less.

I am sturdied by the prospect of less.

Less *in* more.

~~Restlessness~~

~~Sometimes, upon reflection, days feel difficult and stunted and frustrating.~~ Today I feel unsettled, restless, and lacking sturdiness.

I have ~~everything I need in this world and more:~~ shelter, safety, food, family, fulfilling paid work, and volunteerism. ~~(I'm practically dancing on the summit of Maslow's pyramid, baby!)~~

~~Yet, my eye twitch has returned.~~

An unmet ~~need, no matter how deeply ingrained, is undoubtedly~~ restless. ~~There is something askew,~~ something missing.

~~Also, I'm certain I'm not the only one with an itch because scratchy solutions are promised everywhere: promises from highly targeted and cleverly crafted ads on mass and social media, a buffet of ever-evolving tools, tricks, and courses available on demand.~~

~~But I know, deep down,~~ *that the something* can't be solved by any outside means ~~or by anyone other than myself. In my 37 years on planet Earth, I'm only beginning to understand that solutions to complex problems come not from having more answers, but from~~ asking more questions. ~~Solutions are often found by talking less and~~ *listening more.* ~~Solutions make themselves known not through trying to control a situation, but by believing with unwavering conviction that~~ *connection is the ultimate goal.*

but knowing that there's so much more to know.

Without fail, capturing *the something.*

are stillness, less.

- *Becoming Minimalist*
-
- *Letters From Love* finding a sense of calm?"

on my to-do list for years.

fear, an outstretched hand towards internal stillness. asking questions, listening to the answers, and striving for connection, *I know very little.*

in hopes that we may connect— shared restlessness. sturdiness of connection, sliver of stillness.

Dear Love,

Gratitude

Breathe in. That's gratitude.

overcomplicating the process,

breathe. In and out,

For this, I am grateful.

Stillness

~~The ebbing is just as much a part of the process as flowing.~~

Sit, still, settled.

Love is found in stillness.

~~The simplest, yet most difficult thing is moving ahead by not moving.~~

Be still.

~~03/16/21~~

~~There is a deep~~ restlessness ~~inside. Moving, churning, itching for more. You want to close your eyes, bringing~~ stillness ~~to the end of the day.~~

~~Guilt will pass. Forgiveness will come.~~

In the stillness. In the stillness.

~~Don't consume, be consumed.~~

Be still, ~~just rest, for tomorrow is another glorious, hope-filled day.~~

~~Goodnight.~~

An empty crayon box isn't just an empty crayon box.
It becomes a vessel for something new. Making space
is what allows for new possibilities to emerge.

No Map Required

May we follow the direction of our creative compass

In 2011, I quit my day job to figure out what was next. I'd been working in the industry I studied to work in since 2007 when I hit my quarter-life crisis. Hard. (Nobody talks about this, but I assure you it's a real thing.)

Although I enjoyed the outcome of my work (books, books, books!), something wasn't right. As difficult as the decision was to make, I knew it was time to move on; my creative compass (a term I wouldn't discover for a decade) encouraged me to explore a new direction.

Folding Pants

Although I had some money in my savings account and I was living relatively modestly, I wanted to ensure that I had all of my bases covered, which meant getting a job to tide me over before my next career move. So, for the first time in my 10-year working life, I dipped my toes into the retail space.

There aren't many people out there who say that working retail is a great gig. You work long hours on your feet, doing repetitive tasks for relatively little pay. I was determined to secure the best retail gig I could find, and I landed at lululemon. (They actually didn't want to hire me and rejected me on the spot, but I talked them into it—a story for another day.)

Their focus on employee self-development is admirable, and I genuinely enjoyed my time working there, but at the end of the day I realized the job mainly involved folding pants. Simultaneously, I'd never felt more fulfilled creatively in my life.

How? Why?

Before and after my shifts I was building my small business, my creative compass continuing to quietly guide my path. For the first time in a long time, I had the space and desire to focus on creating something for myself, where I could run with a new idea in a relatively low-stakes capacity, kneading it into something bigger than myself.

First Aid

I absolutely love my teaching career today, but there's nothing like the excitement, anticipation, and initial big wins of creating something from nothing. It's the hardest I'd worked in my life, yet it rarely felt like work. I was starting a first aid and CPR training business that had nothing to do with what I went to school for, but rather it's what I had done throughout my teenage years, having worked in a pool environment as a lifeguard and swimming instructor. I had complete creative control with pages and pages and pages full of ideas for things to do, people to call, and ways to grow my humble little enterprise.

After quitting and receiving a nudge of encouragement from my former-boss, I decided to go all in on my new/old venture. In a few short months, I managed to secure my first corporate clients, yoga studios which were a natural fit given my day job at lululemon.

Before I knew it, I had enough clients to say goodbye to the retail world, making almost as much as I had in my previous day job. In just a few short years, I would train over 2,500 people in small group settings across a diverse range of industries. From yoga instructors to truck drivers, primary school students to new parents, I had never before worked with so many diverse people in so many new places.

In hindsight, this time period was a teaching masterclass in helping me prepare for my current career as a full-time lecturer. I had taken a step in the direction pointed by my compass, a knowing rooted deep in my gut.

Finding Flow

Looking back on this time, I realize that I was experiencing what renowned psychologist Mihaly Csikszentmihalyi calls "flow." Flow is a highly focused mental state that requires concentration on the activity at hand. Nothing else seems to matter in moments of intensely focused flow, which can often be experienced when pursuing something athletic or artistic.

Time seems to pass with great speed, and before you know it, hours have gone by. Mihaly believes that people are happiest in a state of flow. During his life, he was interviewed extensively about this important concept, and this is how he explained flow in an interview with *Wired* magazine: "[flow is] being completely involved in an activity for its own sake. The ego falls away. Time flies. Every action, movement, and thought follows inevitably from the previous one, like playing jazz. Your whole being is involved, and you're using your skills to the utmost."[53]

The phrase "time flies when you're having fun" turns out to have scientific merit. (In fact, I think I'm currently in a state of flow with writing. The last time I looked up from my computer it was 11:59 a.m...it's now 12:45 p.m.)

This (this!) is the feeling my creative compass was helping me navigate.

Your Creative Compass

The next step on the journey doesn't require a detailed map or turn-by-turn GPS directions (or if you're a '90s kid, a MapQuest print out). Instead, author Adam Grant reminds us that we only need a compass to help point us in the direction of our core values and then our intuition can take the reins.[54] Even when it feels like we're not ready, by following our compass, we're not only giving ourselves over to the process and possibilities of what could be, but we're also demonstrating to those around us that they can do the same.

Even when it feels like we're not ready, by following our compass, we're not only giving ourselves over to the process and possibilities of what could be, but we're also demonstrating to those around us that they can do the same.

One of the fastest and most effective ways to establish your creative compass is through an activity I like to call "Emoji Eulogy."

I suggest picking up your phone, opening your text messages, and beginning a new text thread with yourself. Identify three emojis that represent how you want to be remembered at the end of your life (grim, but helpful). Your emoji eulogy helps clarify what's most important to you in "your one wild and precious life."[55]

Before choosing your emojis, ask yourself:
- What are some keywords you'd use to describe yourself?
- What's most important to you in this world?
- What would you say are your greatest strengths?
- How do you hope to make others around you feel when you're with them?
- At the end of your life, how do you hope others will describe you?

Once you've answered these questions, pair your responses with emojis. Articulate the *why* behind your choices, explaing (to yourself) what they represent. No one else has to understand or agree with your choices. This is YOUR emoji eulogy: a visual expression of your values that gives shape to your creative compass. While it's impossible to have a life map that dictates your exact journey, it *is* possible to have a compass to guide the direction of travel. Allow this emoji eulogy to act as a compass inviting clarity, acting as a filter, and reminding you of your core values each step of the way. Your decisions moving forward can be less in your head and more in your gut and in your heart.

Once you've identified your whys, it becomes much easier to make day-to-day choices about the what, when, where, who, and how of creative living. In doing so, you can have greater confidence that you're traveling the path that makes sense *for* you (even if it doesn't make sense *to* you yet).

The Moment is Right (Now)

And here's the great news: you don't have to walk the same creative path I did to find feelings of flow that your creative compass is yearning for. Simply create. Create for creation's sake, on your own terms. We don't always need to worry about the end product; instead, focus on the process because the act of making—and who we become during the making—facilitates growth. As authors Jeremy Utley and Perry Klebahn articulate in their book *Ideaflow: The Only Business Metric That Matters,* there's a direct correlation between quantity and quality when it comes to ideas. There's magic to be found in the making, with the bonus that more practice enables growth, improving the ability of our compass to guide us and help us access a state of flow rooted in the present.

The present moment is all any of us have, which is both exciting and terrifying. From a creative perspective, the present moment is especially interesting because never before and never again will there be the exact same conditions that exist right now.

- You've never had as much knowledge as you do right now.
- You've never had as much experience, as much collective wisdom, and as much emotional intelligence as you do right now.
- You'll never again be in the same room with the same people and the same thoughts (and even the same weather outside!) as you are RIGHT NOW.
- The conditions under which you create are as unique as your creations, so take advantage and absorb the thrill of making something in this moment even if you're not ready or you're not sure where you're headed.

Let your creative intuition be your guide. No turn-by-turn directions required.

Let your creative intuition be your guide. No turn-by-turn directions required.

Let your creative intuition be your guide. No turn-by-turn directions required.

Equally exciting and terrifying, you get to draw your own map—no straight lines required. With a crayon in hand, you get to make it up as you go. Take comfort in knowing you're not alone in the uncertainty of drawing your map. We're all navigating our journeys in real time.

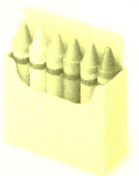

You Are Magical

You are a brave creative human

I don't believe that creative confidence is something you can master; rather, it's a type of magic—something you can learn to cultivate and call upon deep within yourself when you need it most.

The creative confidence journey is never-ending, but it gets easier with time, practice, and patience for yourself when Failure walks alongside you.

You're brave.

Bravery is about showing up with an energy that is open to whatever is on the other side of the unknown. Trust yourself and trust the process because *you've got this.*

You're creative.

The world needs your work, your experiences, and your unique points of view. Give yourself permission to play. Make something uniquely you. Without a doubt, *you've got this.*

You're human.

And they're human, too, on the other side of the table, the Zoom link, the social media feed. From one human to another, *you've got this.*

You are a Brave Creative Human.

GRATE
AND N

TUDE
TES

A BIG
Thank You

It takes a village

Thank you to the advanced reading team of this book (Peter Ha, Michael Young, Chris Rouleau, Nat Lumby) who generously shared their time to provide me with helpful, poignant feedback.

Thank you to the one and only, Guy Anabella, for your outpouring of love on this project and for your beautiful words that begin this book.

Thank you to my incredible, patient, and supportive editor, Mandy Bayrami, for your thoughtful suggestions and detailed edits.

Thank you to my friend, Scott Millward, for your on-call tech help and calm reassurance when I needed it most.

Thank you, Laura Brady, for your technical ebook and accessibility wizardry, enabling a fully-equipped digital version of this work to exist.

Thank you to the brave creative humans who gifted me time to tap into their unique selves in an audio format in advance of this book's publication (Emad Saedi, Meg Lewis, Vincent Wanga, Ally MacKenzie, Justine Abigail Yu, Kevin Shaw).

Thank you to the workshoppers of my Domestika Building Creative Confidence course (Paul Twa, Nat Lumby, Chris Ambedkar, Nikita Kuzmin, Veronika Wiszniewska, Samir Mackai, Sadya Haque, Sarah Wright, Suzie Menendez, Olivia Mule, Akanksha Sharma, Michelle Callegari, and conversations with many others) who helped me grow my ideas to expand them in new directions, many of which have become the basis for this book.

Thank you to the RGD team, as well as to the RGD community at-large. What a wonderful place to collaborate with like-minded folks! It's a space that's connected me with others who have allowed me to share, articulate, and incubate perspective-shifting ideas.

Thank you 2G2G for always being in my corner, creatively and otherwise.

Thank you, Adam, for your unending support of all my side quests, and for your big humour and bigger heart.

Thank you to my kiddos for their endless love of play and making, consistently fueling my brave creative humanity.

Notes

Sources, sites, specifics

Endnotes

INTRODUCTION

1. Oxford Learner's Dictionaries, s.v. "Creativity." Accessed May 16, 2025, https://www.oxfordlearnersdictionaries.com/us/definition/english/creativity?q=creativity

2. Bowler, Maria. *Making Time: A New Vision for Crafting a Life beyond Productivity.* Grand Rapids, MI: Baker Publishing Group, 2025, 165.

3. Oxford Learner's Dictionaries, s.v. "Confidence." Accessed May 16, 2025, https://www.oxfordlearnersdictionaries.com/us/definition/english/confidence?q=confidence

4. Doyle, Glennon. "How to Raise Untamed Kids with Dr. Becky Kennedy," *We Can Do Hard Things.* Produced by Allison Schott, Dynna Cabana and Lauren LoGrasso. Accessed May 14, 2025. https://wecandohardthingspodcast.com/.

5. Kim, Kyung Hee, and Robert A. Pierce. "Convergent versus Divergent Thinking." *Encyclopedia of Creativity, Invention, Innovation and Entrepreneurship,* 2013, 245–50. https://doi.org/10.1007/978-1-4614-3858-8_22.

6. Robinson, Ken. "Do Schools Kill Creativity?" *TED Talk*, February 2006. Video 6:06, https://www.ted.com/talks/sir_ken_robinson_do_schools_kill_creativity/transcript?subtitle=en.

BRAVE

7 Kent, Corita, and Steward, Jan. *Learning by Heart: Teachings to Free the Creative Spirit*. New York: Allworth Press, 2008, 1.

8 Attributed to Simon Sinek. "People who wonder whether the glass is half empty or half full miss the point. The glass is refillable." Accessed May 16, 2025. https://www.goodnewsnetwork.org/simon-sinek-quote-about-glass-half-full/.

9 Godin, Seth. *The Practice: Shipping Creative Work*. New York: Portfolio/Penguin, 2020, 23.

10 Godin, Seth. *The Practice: Shipping Creative Work*. New York: Portfolio/Penguin, 2020, 28.

11 Portman, Natalie. "Natalie Portman Harvard Commencement Speech | Harvard Commencement 2015" YouTube video, May 27, 2015. 1:04, https://www.youtube.com/watch?v=jDaZu_KEMCY.

12 Strayed, Cheryl. "A Conversation with Cheryl Strayed." Interview by Ashley Petry. BOOTH, July 25, 2014. https://booth.butler.edu/2014/07/25/a-conversation-with-cheryl-strayed/.

13 Gross, Terry. "Tom Hanks: *Fresh Air*." Produced by WHYY-FM. NPR. Podcast, 00:03:53. https://www.npr.org/transcripts/475573489.

14 Nyong'o, Lupita. "Lupita Nyong'o: 'If I'm having a Cinderella moment, why not enjoy the hell out of it?'" Interview by Tom Huddleston. TimeOut, September 26, 2016. https://www.timeout.com/film/lupita-nyongo-if-im-having-a-cinderella-moment-why-not-enjoy-the-hell-out-of-it.

15 Brown, Brené. *Atlas of the Heart: Mapping Meaningful Connection and the Language of Human Experience.* New York: Random House, 2021, 20.

16 Clear, James. *Atomic Habits: An Easy and Proven Way to Build Good Habits and Break Bad Ones.* New York: Avery, 2018, 92-93.

17 Brown, Brené. *Atlas of the Heart: Mapping Meaningful Connection and the Language of Human Experience.* New York: Random House, 2021, 20.

18 Godin, Seth. *The Practice: Shipping Creative Work.* New York: Portfolio, 2020, 256.

19 "History Timeline: Post-it® Notes." *3M.* Accessed May 16, 2025. https://www.post-it.com/3M/en_US/post-it/contact-us/about-us/.

20 *Oxford Learner's Dictionaries,* s.v. "failure." Accessed May 16, 2025, https://www.oxfordlearnersdictionaries.com/definition/english/failure.

21 *Etymonline,* s.v. "failure." Accessed May 16, 2025, https://www.etymonline.com/word/failure.

22 Godin, Seth. *The Icarus Deception: How High Will You Fly?* New York: Portfolio, 2012.

23 Gilbert, Elizabeth. "Your elusive creative genius." *TED Talk*, February 2009, Video 6:08. https://www.ted.com/talks/elizabeth_gilbert_your_elusive_creative_genius?language=en.

24 Karim, Jawad. "Jawed Karim, Illinois Commencement 2007, pt2." YouTube video, June 5, 2007. https://www.youtube.com/watch?v=24yglUYbKXE.

25 Ricci, Talia. "YouTube celebrates 20th anniversary milestone." CBC. May 2, 2025. https://www.cbc.ca/news/canada/youtube-anniversary-milestone-1.7521783.

26 Elkins, Kathleen. "How much money you need to be among the richest 10 percent of people worldwide." CNBC Money. November 7, 2018. https://owl.purdue.edu/owl/research_and_citation/chicago_manual_17th_edition/cmos_formatting_and_style_guide/web_sources.html.

27 Attributed to Jim Carey. "I wish everyone could get rich and famous and everything they ever dreamed of so they can see that's not the answer." Accessed May 16, 2025. https://x.com/librarymindset/status/1541035585627779072.

28 Brickman, Philip, Dan Coates, and Ronnie Janoff-Bulman. "Lottery Winners and Accident Cictims: Is Happiness Relative?" *Journal of Personality and Social Psychology, 36* (8), (1978), 917–927. https://doi.org/10.1037/0022-3514.36.8.917.

29 García, Héctor, and Francesc Miralles. *Ikigai: The Japanese Secret to a Long and Happy Life.* Translated by Heather Cleary. New York: Penguin Books, 2017.

30 "Welcome to the Harvard Study of Adult Development". *Harvard.* Accessed May 16, 2025. https://www.adultdevelopmentstudy.org/.

31 Adeney, Peter. "Happiness is the Only Logical Pursuit." *Mr. Money Moustache.* June 8, 2016. https://www.mrmoneymustache.com/2016/06/08/happiness-is-the-only-logical-pursuit/comment-page-2/.

32 Coelho, Paulo. "1 MIN READING: The Fisherman and the Businessman." *Stories & Reflections,* 2021. https://

paulocoelhoblog.com/2015/09/04/the-fisherman-and-the-businessman/.

33 Yeager, Jeff. *The Cheapskate Next Door: The Surprising Secrets of Americans Living Happily Below Their Means.* New York: Crown, 2010.

34 Attributed to Dave Ramsey. "We buy things we don't need with money we don't have to impress people we don't like." Accessed May 16, 2025. https://www.instagram.com/reel/C_s8GOGuqT2/.

35 "Total Household Debt Reaches $16.90 trillion in Q4 2022; Mortgage and Auto Loan Growth Slows." *Federal Reserve Bank of New York.* February 16, 2023. https://www.newyorkfed.org/newsevents/news/research/2023/20230216.

CREATIVE

36 @timescanner. "Be a Kermit the Frog. Have a creative vision and no ego. Recognize the unique talents of those around you. Attract weirdos. Manage chaos. Show kindness. Be sincere." Twitter post, August 16, 2022, 2:24 a.m. https://x.com/timescanner/status/1559425751450996736?lang=en

37 McNee, Amie. "The secret life of YOUR art," *Amie's substack* (blog), March 9, 2025, https://amiemcnee.substack.com/p/the-secret-life-of-your-art.

38 Doyle, Glennon. "ALOK: How do we interrupt trauma? How do we heal?" Produced by Allison Schott, Dynna Cabana and Lauren LoGrasso. *We Can Do Hard Things.* Podcast, 23:23. https://wecandohardthingspodcast.com/.

39 Chida, Brit (@britchida). "I am not an initiative or

a project that can be a success or failure. I am part of nature that gets to be 'alive for a little while.'" Instagram, January 21, 2024. https://www.instagram.com/p/C2Y6RDtr_sv/?img_index=1.

40 Goddard, Gertie. "Biomimetic design: 10 examples of nature inspiring technology." *BBC Science Focus*. Accessed on May 16, 2025. https://www.sciencefocus.com/future-technology/biomimetic-design-10-examples-of-nature-inspiring-technology.

41 Moor, Lisandra. "Japanese Words We Can't Translate: Mono no Aware." *Tokyo Weekender*, June 26, 2020. https://www.tokyoweekender.com/art_and_culture/japanese-culture/japanese-words-translate-mono-no-aware/.

42 Attributed to Yves Klein. "My paintings are only the ashes of my art." Accessed June 10, 2025. https://www.sothebys.com/en/auctions/ecatalogue/2012/the-gunter-sachs-collection-evening-auction/lot.4.html.

43 Godin, Seth. The Practice: Shipping Creative Work. New York: Portfolio, 2020, 256.

44 Gilbert, Elizabeth. *Big Magic: Creative Living Beyond Fear.* New York: Riverhead, 2016.

45 Jaouad, Suleika. "Transcript: A Creative Heart-to-Heart with Jon Batiste and Suleika Jaouad." Interview by Suleika Jaouad. *The Isolation Journals*, February 13, 2022. https://theisolationjournals.substack.com/p/transcript-a-creative-heart-to-heart.

46 *Cambridge Dictionary*, s.v. "certainty." Accessed June 8, 2025. https://dictionary.cambridge.org/dictionary/english/certainty.

HUMAN

47 Novogratz, Jacqueline (@jnovogratz), "What if we measured true success not by the amount of money you have but by the amount of human energy you unlock, the amount of potential you enable? If that were our metric, our world would be a different place." Twitter post, August 31, 2019, 12:59 p.m.

48 *Cambridge Dictionary,* s.v. "perfection." Accessed June 8, 2025. https://dictionary.cambridge.org/dictionary/english/perfection.

49 Congdon, Lisa. "The Magic of the Space Between: Embracing the Messy Middle." Presentation at *DesignThinkers Vancouver 2024,* Vancouver, BC, May 28-29, 2024.

50 Ward, Alie. "Attention-Deficit Neuropsychology (ADHD) Part 2 with How to ADHD, Black Girl Lost Keys, Jahla Osborne + more." Produced by Alie Ward. *Ologies with Alie Ward.* Podcast, 01:28:25. https://www.alieward.com/ologies/adhd2.

51 Attributed to Bob Marley. "The day you stop racing, is the day you win the race." Accessed June 10, 2025. https://www.goodreads.com/quotes/357227-the-day-you-stop-racing-is-the-day-you-win.

52 Psychology Today Staff. "Frequency Illusion." *Psychology Today.* June 3, 2025. https://www.psychologytoday.com/ca/basics/frequency-illusion.

53 Geirland, John. "Go With The Flow." *Wired.* September 1, 1996. https://www.wired.com/1996/09/czik/.

54 Adam Grant creative compass reference needed Adam Grant, "Big career decisions don't come with a map,

but all you need is a compass." LinkedIn post, 2022. https://www.linkedin.com/posts/adammgrant_big-career-decisions-dont-come-with-a-map-activity-6914581932894756864-gjzH/.

55 Oliver, Mary. "Poem 133: The Summer Day." Library of Congress. Accessed June 10, 2025. https://www.loc.gov/programs/poetry-and-literature/poet-laureate/poet-laureate-projects/poetry-180/all-poems/item/poetry-180-133/the-summer-day/

GRATITUDE & NOTES

56 Amazon Kindle Direct Publishing. "Print Options." June 2025. https://kdp.amazon.com/en_US/help/topic/G201834180.

57 Amazon Kindle Direct Publishing Community. "Do Paperbacks Print in Canada for Amazon.ca Prime Customers?" June 2025. https://www.kdpcommunity.com/s/question/0D52T00005AQ13BSAT/do-paperbacks-print-in-canada-for-amazonca-prime-customers?language=en_US.

58 Naomi Blumberg, "colophon." *Britannica*. June 2024, https://www.britannica.com/art/colophon-visual-arts.

Photo Credits

Lending visuals to words

Digital drawings created by Charlotte (age 8) and Hannah (age 6).

A big thank you to the *Thiings* team for access to all of the delightful icons throughout this project.

Diana's headshot by Emily Krbec, 2021.

Guy Anabella's headshot by Quinton Cruickshanks (@_qweenton), 2025.

Unless otherwise stated, all photos are public domain or considered fair use.

About the Author

Diana Varma, Curious Human

Diana Varma works as a design educator at Toronto Metropolitan University by day and a podcaster by night—getting creative with creatives about all things creative. She is a curious human who dabbles in a variety of printing technologies and currently serves as VP of Education on the Board of Directors for the RGD, Canada's largest professional association for graphic designers. Diana lives with her family near Toronto.

This book pairs beautifully with Diana's Domestika course, *Building Creative Confidence: Unleash Your Potential.* Continue your creative confidence journey with videos and experiential exercises, culminating in the creation of your creative manifesto.

www.talkpaperscissors.info

Instagram @talkpaperscissors

Colophon

You can take the teacher out of the classroom, but you can't take the classroom out of the teacher...

The moment I've been waiting for...time to get geeky!

Here are production notes from the making of *Brave Creative Human*.

Fonts:
- WTR Gothic Open Shaded (Wood Type Revival via Adobe Fonts)
- Ed's Market (Laura Worthington Type via Adobe Fonts)
- Impact Label (Tension Type via Font Space)
- Minion Pro (Robert Slimbach for Adobe Originals via Adobe Fonts)
- Polymath (OH no Type Co. via Adobe Fonts)
- Proxima Nova (Mark Simonson Studio via Adobe Fonts)

Software:
- Cover: Adobe Illustrator 28.7.1 (2024)
- Internal Pages: Adobe InDesign 20.3.1 (2025)
- Illustrations: Procreate 5.3.15 version (Apple iPad and Pencil)
- Brush: Crayon Brushes for Procreate (Wink Brushes via Creative Market)

Paper:
- Cover: 80 lb. (220 GSM) white paper stock
- Internal Pages: Black ink and 50-61 lb. (74-90 GSM) cream paper (and according to Amazon Kindle Direct Publishing: "paper weight varies based on printing location."[56])

Printing Process:
- The printed version of this book is manufactured digitally print-on-demand (POD) by Kindle Direct Publishing (KDP).
- This means that only when an order is placed does production (of that single copy of the book) begin. According to the KDP community at the time of writing, Amazon KDP prints and distributes paperback books to Canadian readers in a facility in Bolton, Ontario.[57]

Final Nerdy Note:

If you're wondering about the origins of the colophon itself, Encyclopaedia Britannica specifies that it refers to the information placed at the end of a manuscript or book that provides details about publishing, including the scribe's name, the name of the printer, the date of printing, and other important production information. Colophons were included in books as early as 6th century CE. Typically the colophon exists today as a single line on the copyright page of a book, stating the name and location of the printing company that manufactured it.[58] I gleefully continue the tradition of the back-page colophon (nay, three back pages!), adding a modern digital graphic communications spin, providing information about the fonts and design software used.

www.ingramcontent.com/pod-product-compliance
Lightning Source LLC
Chambersburg PA
CBHW010248010526
44119CB00055B/773